The Common Sense

What to Write, How to Write It, and Why

The
Common Sense

*What to Write,
How to Write It,
and Why*

ROSEMARY DEEN AND MARIE PONSOT

BOYNTON/COOK PUBLISHERS
HEINEMANN
PORTSMOUTH, NH

Acknowledgments

We gratefully acknowledge the following:

The Fundamental Skills Committee of the University of Massachusetts/Boston, for permission to use questions from their Proficiency Examination.

"The Span of Life" and "Nothing Gold Can Stay" from *The Poetry of Robert Frost* edited by Edward Connery Lathem. Copyright 1923, © 1969 by Holt, Rinehart and Winston. Copyright 1936, 1951 by Robert Frost. Copyright © 1964 by Lesley Frost Ballantine. Reprinted by permission of Holt, Rinehart and Winston.

Boynton/Cook Publishers Inc.
A subsidiary of Reed Elsevier Inc.
361 Hanover Street   Portsmouth, NH   03801-3912
Offices and agents throughout the world

Library of Congress Cataloging in Publication Data

Deen, Rosemary.
   The common sense.

   Includes index.
   1. English language—Rhetoric. 2. Essay. 3. Report writing.
4. Exposition (Rhetoric) I. Ponsot, Marie.
II. Title
PE1471.D43   1985   808'.042   85-4126
ISBN 0-86709-079-0

Printed in the United States of America
99 98   DA   9 10 11

Preface

This is a brief book teaching the elements of writing inductively, by organized experience; and concentrating the practice of writing on the expository essay, the essay which supports what it asserts. It's brief because it's elemental: it makes choices; and because it's inductive: the experience comes first and contains its reasons.

You can use the book for four kinds of expository writing courses. Designs for two of them are in the appendix. The most beautiful course, which underlies the others, is "Elements of the Essay." It suits inexperienced writers of all ages; or writers who want to practice all the elements of writing in a developing way; or mixed groups of writers. It has been used successfully by experienced and by brand-new teachers. It's the single most radically instructive thing in the book.

The second course, "Two-Part Essay Shapes", teaches the essay by beginning with classic forms. These shape both source literature, like autobiography, and satire and analytic literature. That's why there's no divide in the span of literature and no big cross-over from familiar essay to analysis in student writing. You'll find an overview of the six essay shapes, showing both literary and analytic types, on page 88.

Both the third and fourth courses include analysis of outside texts. The third brings in three or four pieces of literature as genre types; the fourth is entirely writing about literature. Any teacher who loves language and literature will be at home in our courses because we've drawn them from our sense that expository writing is important. It's not second-rate writing, nor is teaching it second-rate work.

The expository essay can be defined dialectically as something whose mockery is the five-paragraph theme, made mechanically from the top down beginning with a topic sentence and ending with what Bob Boynton calls "rephrasing the thesis in embossed tones." But, "a telling expository essay moves from the inside out, as does all literature." All writing in this book begins with a concrete center, the writers' observations, data, or sense of the shape of their experience. Out of this, by writing and rewriting, writers abstract their first definition of their idea. As they write and rewrite, the idea organizes the data from which it came; and, at the same time, the data tests and refines its definition.

We find the term "writing process" as distasteful as the term "creative writing" when "creative" is reserved for poetry, drama, story. Writing is energy and act. Because it is act, writing is a power to be exercised. Rewriting (real not remedial) is the central, writer's way to fluency and structure. But it's hard to teach. Though rewriting is almost an instinct with real writers, it was the most stubborn of our teaching discoveries. Those who have tried to teach it instead of forcing it on students will find this book useful.

The subtitle of the book tells its organization. "What to Write" is the structures and forms implied in our directions for writing. "What" is directions because learning is inductive and empirical. We mean every word and every metaphor in every word we say; that's what makes the book bridge the range of users. There's no concealed text. It's doing *what* we say and *all* we say that works.

The directions lay out a core of work that can't be done wrong. That puts you on the side of writers, makes you their ally instead of their accuser. "You can't do it wrong" means what it says. It's not just reassurance and support. We're not interested in what our students *feel*, but in what they do. Our research consisted of finding out what could be taught directly and inductively by anyone with good will and plenty of experience with literature. Only elements can be taught. Only work that doesn't leave writers' strengths behind keeps on working. We wanted to give students a reality, even if it was a small one, that would demonstrate its existence by developing differently in every writer, develop without our knowing it ahead of time, and without our always being there to coax it out.

"How to Write It" is learned by writing, listening, and writing observations. The sample essays show how some of our writers wrote. They are not models, and for that reason they come at the end of the book. Sample observations follow some of the essays.

The hardest part of this book for us was writing inductively to teach writing inductively. Confining ourselves to directions and definitions, and making our chapters as brief and elemental as possible, were our ways of keeping the promise of induction. The "Why" of the book, then, is its definitions, the minimum explanation we could manage. Definitions appear *after* directions and are indexed at the end of the book. Because this book works inductively, we hope it will also be used by people who want to write, need other writers, and don't have teachers. The first four short chapters explain this possibility.

Beginning with the shapes of literature teaches organization and development. And the ability to develop is telling: it tells who's in charge. "Literature" implies that writers originate their ideas, and that ideas, which are "generative seeds," must be thoroughly imagined by their authors in order to speak to others. Writing to imagine the idea, getting it into the mind and out onto the page, is the work whose elements this book sorts out and puts in good order for writers.

For the teachers:

Sr. Aquin Gallagher, O.P.
Alma Walsh

Contents

PART ONE

Elements of the Essay

1

Why Write?

You're thinking about staking a claim to the powerful energies of writing. Why should you bother?

Why write?

It's a real question. Some of the traditional advantages of writing well no longer come exclusively from that skill. For instance, we write to record what's memorable, both to remind ourselves of it and to give it life outside our time. We write to transmit data efficiently, to give it a life outside our local place. Yes; but we can also use telephones, films, computers, tapes, etc., to extend the reach and remembrance of what we have to say. For saving and transmitting information, we can replace the low-cost efficiency of writing by as many technologies as we can afford and manipulate. Some possibilities once realized by written language may now be met by spoken language, electronically conveyed.

We writers welcome electronic devices and anything else that extends the presence of language, knowing we can take care that the language we give them to present is implicit with the ordered power of thought.

Still, there are reasons for writing. Here are two small ones:

First, for those who know how to play when writing, it's lots of fun, a self-renewing game with no time pressure, no expensive equipment, and no loser.

Second, writing can get information out of well-informed machines and well-stocked libraries and into our heads where we need it. Of the two good ways to absorb data, one is listening; about a third of us learn well that way. The other is writing in our own hand: copying data, taking notes, rereading and recopying; two-thirds of us learn well this way. (Try it yourself. Write a formula or a couple of lines of a poem; copy it attentively, twice. Then see if you can write it from memory the third time.) These, however, are among the many peripheral powers of writing, remote in comparison with its central use.

The use of writing is thinking. Writing does not so much teach us to think or require us to plan to think, as it does help us to think with and through it as we do it.

In writing we call on tremendous human energies, impacted

in language. The thinking self is drawn into view, in expression that can be re-viewed, re-written, re-cast, cut, developed, and worked on, a day or a decade later. By its very physicality, writing brings us as close as we ever come to handling our ideas. It draws out thought to where it becomes material for further thought, ready to change or go forward from. What the writing finally says will be personal to the writer and may well be original. Better, it can be changed until it says something the writer is willing to stand responsible for.

As we write, we can uncover in our minds new ideas to order and new kinds of order, too. What we uncover often surprises us, though we come to count on such surprise. Writing is a wily agent of discovery. The mental acts of energy behind it are in good part as involuntary as breath, but they come under conscious control as we make them visible and malleable on the page. Writing enables us to see and show what we think. It encourages us to press against the bounds of what we know, by giving us the pleasure of the made and the found.

2

Writing: The Expository Essay

The elements of writing well can be taught and learned because they can be identified and practiced. The elements work together, so that learning to write gives the reinforcing pleasure natural to acquiring a skill.

This book identifies a set of five elements and shows exactly what writing you can do to practice them. They are: writing concretely and abstractly; writing from generative structures; writing observations as distinguished from inferences; writing fluently and prolifically; and rewriting. The elements of skilled writing are always the same. They can be practiced in more and other ways than we set out, of course; what we propose here is a minimal number of moves to rehearse for success.

The skill rising from these five elements underlies the making of literature of all kinds—drama, fiction, poetry, nonfiction prose. Each of these genres has its own requirements and techniques; and each can be divided more narrowly, in various ways, into kinds. (Among poems, for instance, there are lyrics, narratives, epics, etc.; there are sonnets, ballads, sestinas, etc.; there are satires, hymns of praise, aubades, etc.) Chapters 1–10 present the five skills elemental to all kinds of writing. After that, the ways to practice the skills which we present in this book lead most efficiently to writing nonfiction prose.

The kind of nonfiction prose the book works toward is the essay. The kind of essay it asks you to practice is still narrower: the essay of exposition.

An expository essay is one which supports the idea it asserts. It exposes (*exposui*: I have put forth) the writer's demonstration or proof of an idea generated by the writer's knowledge of concrete data. It exposes the writer's idea in terms of the supporting information from which it has risen.

The academic version of the expository essay is most often practiced in English Composition classes. It is then performed in other disciplines and areas. One characteristic particular to good academic exposition is the noticeable ordering and division of its parts. Another is fluency of development. This book gives you occasions to practice both.

Putting forth support for your ideas gives you exercise in mastering the information you're studying. You master it by using the data you learn: first, to generate and express an idea; and second, to order the data into a reasonably developed support. What the mind has used, it tends to remember. Academic exposition is the place where you can extend and exhibit such mastery of a subject as you have achieved.

Within academic life, it's rare that students in, say, a medieval history course will write about an idea based on new or original data. To learn data as given is the primary work of the course. The instructor who asks you to write papers expects you to show that you do, indeed, have the data well enough in mind to be able to (1) think about the data, (2) generate an idea about the data, (3) express the idea amply, and (4) order the data to support the idea. Since all writing is an ordering of what the writer has in mind, academic exposition gives you two useful chances at mastering a subject: first, to think more about and remember actively your data; and second, to have an idea closely drawn from the data, which shows others how fruitful your studies have been.

Successful papers need not depend on luck or a canny guess at what an instructor wants. A more certain and earned success depends on knowing how to write an expository essay, alive and recognizable anywhere.

This book tells you what to do, to be ready, willing and able to do justice to your learning by writing about it with pleasure, appropriately and well.

3

Community for a Group of Writers

You've decided to work at writing well. Here you are, looking into a book on writing: Will it serve you? You notice it talks about working with a group. But writing may seem to you to be a solo act. It is. Then, can a group change your writing for the better? Yes. You can learn together, and from each other, to write better on your own.

This book proposes economical and powerful work which will steadily develop your skill without any waste of time.

One vital way to use time well is to engage in the multiple teaching/learning exchange of work planned for each person in a group, working together. You'll learn more, more rapidly, deeper, than you would working alone. You'll have the expanding richness and ease that a variety of minds produces.

If you're in a class, some of the logistical needs of a working community have been organized for you. A class is a group of people who've chosen something they want to learn, and have been given, for fifteen weeks or so, an expert, a time, and a place in which to learn it. This book takes advantage of that situation. It sets out a unifying field of work which everyone is able to do more fruitfully together than alone, so that a sense of community unfolds. It is not competitive; it is work by which everyone is helpful to everyone else—without trying and without a moment's distraction from each one's own growth.

Perhaps you've been thinking of working alone, as many of us do when we realize we want to learn something but prefer to get past the awkward beginnings in private. If so, now's the time to find a few acquaintances to join your enterprise. These are beginnings that won't make you awkward.

Our notion of ideal size for writing groups is from, say, 10 minimum to 25 maximum. But if you can get only a few to join you, you'll find that more efficient than working alone or receiving one-on-one tutoring. (Not that the work ahead can't be done alone—it can. But you learn from the constant showing of others' work and from the identifying view many minds will give you of your own.)

We've been in many classes where the flow of attention moved on unbending radii from a teaching center to the minds of students and—when it was succeeding—back again. That is, however, not an efficient design for the democracy of a writing group. This book gives everyone plenty to do so that the group becomes a network of energies, and the classic need of writers for other writers is met. It also frees instructors for their proper tasks, so that their interest and expertise can flourish unexhausted.

Yes, the act of writing is a solo act. To be an author is to have singular authority. But when the writing session is packed with practice, as writers work alongside each other, skills grow. As they grow, their growth accelerates. Someone is always noticeably writing better; the visibility of progress in skill goes unpredictably by leaps. Each member internalizes the dynamism and something of the mental habits of others in the group. Given such reason to hope, all respond to that speeded-up expansion with fresh readiness to practice in their own way, on their own. It helps to see, hear, and take part in what Tara and Evan and John and Julia do, and how they do it. It teaches.

Meanwhile, it meets writers' deep need for a fair hearing, a true audience. Often writers fail to discover the great and equitable art of exposition because they misdirect their papers. They address what they hope are attractive opinions to what they hope they have diagnosed correctly as the prejudices of some fictional audience, perhaps an instructor. They do not present data-supported ideas. They have given up exposition and settled for propaganda.

When members of a group are colleagues, co-laborers, not competitors, they "watch not one another out of fear." They can address their words to reason, to the reasoning power they have identified in each other. They can be responsible for their words. That draws from them the writing proper to their community.

4

What Kind of Book Is This? How Will You Use It?

This book depends on working from strength, your strength. We've never seen a writing book put together this way. So we imagine you too will find it different. Here are some insiders' hints on getting the most good out of it.

1. This book gives you the grounds on which your writing can work out, and the set of things to do that will get your writing into great shape. It's all up to you. The work you do will teach you: if, as, and after you do it. In the process, you will have written your own true textbook.

2. So take your time. Don't waste any. The book doesn't tell you about what good writing is. But you'll be able to produce and recognize it, and describe and define it, out of your own experience. You are the author. The author has authority over the writing. All writing from this book is good authorial practice, so nothing you do is mistaken or a waste of time. This is calming and constructive.

3. Do the work in each chapter right after you read a sentence that asks for it. Paragraphs following the directions refer to things you'll know about because you've done the work. Writing from this book teaches you inductively. This means that it begins with, strengthens, and never abandons powers you already have. It counts on practice making for perfection. These powers, used, identified, and practiced, are your great resource (beyond this book, beyond any books or teachers). They produce writing that thinks with you and speaks for you; writing that is for you, for your life.

4. Do the work chapter by chapter, in order. All of the work is brisk, brief, and keeps you moving along. None of its is hard. None of it can do your writing harm. None of it can be done wrong. (See Chapter 41 for more on this.) Each chapter has consequences in the next chapter and is the consequence of the earlier ones. Writing from this book is consecutive.

5. Don't toss out papers you've written. Date and label them. Keep them to look at again, in the new light later papers provide. Writing from this book is cumulative.

6. Most of the writing has implications which grow clear and

unforgettably useful to you through repetition. So the directions call for writing a number of versions. The number is a minimum! Don't do fewer. Writing from this book uses repetition incrementally.

7. There are a few chapters and notes about matters connected to writing. They are more easily displaceable than the chapters of direct writing. Read them as you come to them. Read them aloud. Keep them in mind. Go back to look at them now and then. Their information will strike you differently as your skill broadens to include more experience of what they offer. They won't change, but you, as a thinking writer, will.

8. To spotlight our stance more sharply, we might say: how you feel about your writing before you start doesn't matter. The power of your language will free you to practice it, since we have sorted out the elemental energies of language into parts which repay practice.

9. How can we make these hopeful claims? We can claim them because, knowing what the teachable elements of writing are, we give you in this book, in good order, good ways to practice them. We trust the structuring power of language—which you have, and the structuring power of the great primal forms of literature—which this book asks you to embody and enjoy attentively.

5

The Fable

Now it's your turn.

It's time, before talking any more about writing, to take 15 or 20 minutes and write. Here's some writing you can do quickly that you can't do wrong. It will give you energy and a concrete experience to draw on.

Start by practicing dialogue. Two characters will have a conversation. To refresh your memory, here are samples of how to punctuate sentences that quote a speaker's exact words:

1. "April is the cruelest month," Tom said. Or: Tom said, "April is the cruelest month." Or: "April," Tom said, "is the cruelest month."
2. Start a new paragraph whenever you finish quoting one speaker or begin to quote another:

   Geoffrey once said, "April with its sweet showers fills every vein with liquor."

   But Tom said, "April is the cruelest month."

The punctuation is useful, for with it you can show who is speaking and where the speaker's words start and stop.

Now, turn your thoughts to the world of imagination. Imagine that it's the middle of the night, in the middle of the countryside, and down the road comes a horse. The horse meets a bear.

For your first paragraph, quickly write what the horse says to the bear. (Do that. Don't go on reading till you've done it.)

For your second paragraph, write what the bear says to the horse.

And, when you've done that, write, for the third paragraph, what the horse says to the bear.

For your fourth paragraph, we'd like a sentence or two that tell something different. Instead of quoting a speaker, write a quick sentence describing a natural event occurring there in the middle of the night in the middle of the road. It may be a minor cataclysm—perhaps a meteor falls, a storm breaks out, or some such sudden change takes place.

That done, for paragraph 5, write what the bear says to the horse.

And, for paragraph 6, the last exchange in this dialogue, write what the horse says to the bear.

Well, there you are: a concrete, written dialogue in hand. Read it over, skip a line, and write, "The moral of this fable is _____ ." Fill in the blank by writing a few morals for your dialogue. Set down at least 3 of them. (It's easier to write 3 than 1, because with only one chance at it, you'll have more trouble deciding what to say.)

Now, if you're one of a group of writers, you'll encounter one of the instructive pleasures writers can offer each other, as you sit back and listen to all the other writers read their fables aloud and you read yours to them.

It's good to know from experience, as you now do, that you can always write a fable. No structure is more handsome, more accessible, or more flexible of aim. People have often disagreed about what literature ought to accomplish; some say it's pure pleasure, some say pure instruction; some say it must mirror life, and some say it's a world all its own. Fable-makers have never had to take sides in such arguments, for fables can't help but delight as they inform and inform as they delight. They're imaginary little worlds, yet reflect something telling about our lives. They take equally well to satire, irony, reflection, wit, or poetry.

You can write a fable on the back of an envelope as you wait for a bus, just for the pleasure of it. You can write some 50 years from now, to convey once and for all an idea of who you are and what you value. One fable is like one grape: it's hard to stop with eating just one, when bunches and bunches more are well within hand's reach—tasty, juicy, and full of energy.

Help yourself! Write 7 or 8 more fables. Use as characters any creatures you like. Use the same structure as the first fable. Begin— not by puzzling out a plot, and certainly not with a moral, but immediately—with dialogue/event/dialogue, which is a concrete drama or story. Finish with the morals, or aphorisms, which are fitting sentences as strong and elegant as you can make them.

Be sure to listen well as you and your colleagues read each new set of fables aloud to each other. The more fables you write and listen to, the more fully you'll sense the strength of the whole structure. By the time you've written and heard your colleagues' 8 or 9, you'll have intuited the dynamics of the 2-part shape. You'll know why every culture in every age has found the fable fabulous.

The pleasure of the fable expands and confirms, through repetition, your power to intuit its structure—so that you'll produce and recognize it without needing to define the way it works. Definition always properly comes after understanding and use (and even then, it's not necessary to them).

6

Rewriting: The Aphorism

Here's another chance to let the structuring power of your language work for you.

From among the aphorisms that your group has written and read along with their fables, choose one you like. Let everyone write it down.

In 5 minutes, write 3 new sentences, each of which conveys more or less the same idea as the aphorism. Use some of the same words if you like, or change them. Elegance is the aim. Make your sentences sound wonderful.

Have everyone read the new versions aloud. You can see at once how fertile syntax is. In no time at all, that aphorism has given rise to dozens of newly expressive sentences. Some of them probably give a new twist to the idea, or take it a step further. All are original and new.

By the way, never think that rewriting is strange or difficult. It's really a natural way to keep your thoughts going. You don't rewrite to remedy mistakes or correct the original—that's copy-editing, which is the final polishing of a finished paper. You rewrite as you create your piece of writing, by exploring your language for what more it can make of your good work. The most basic kind of rewriting is the one you have just done, and it can't be done wrong. Sentence by sentence, you can work on any thought, in any piece of writing, and be sure that your language will bring out more of the best of your idea.

The fable is an especially good place to look at the effect of a well-rewritten sentence, since the shape of the fable depends on the elegance of the aphorism for its strong conclusion. The pleasure of a memorable ending is one of the reasons fables are so satisfying. A final sentence, enclosing and showing the idea which the earlier paragraphs have expressed concretely, gives a sense of completeness and has the power of closure.

Go back to the fables you've written, and for each of them rewrite the aphorism you like best. Three new versions will give you the idea; but don't stop there. See what happens when you aim for 5 or 10. Notice how quickly you and your colleagues pick up especially good sentence shapes from each other.

Remember that whenever your group has a few minutes to spare, you can enrich the time by rewriting a good sentence to see how many fine ways there are to say anything. In fact, given the exhilaration of this kind of play with language, you may find you have a new lifetime pastime: cheap, portable, and worthy both of Milton and of passengers needing distraction on a long car ride.

7

Writing Observations on the Aphorism

Literature belongs partly to its author and partly to its listeners. You've been writing and reading aloud; now change your focus and consider yourself the listener and observer. You have a steady, powerful influence on the writing of your group simply by the way you listen and respond. Here's a way of listening that fits the writing assignments, teaches you the magnificent skill of attention, and encourages the developing writing powers of your group.

Choose one fable from your group's work so far, one you remember. Ask the author to read it again while you enjoy listening to it. Here's a fable as an example:

BEAR AND LION

BEAR: "This is my territiory. I don't need you roaring around here and scaring bees."

LION: "Bees sleep at night. My roars won't wake them up."

BEAR: "You don't think so? Bees are pretty sensitive, you know."

LION: "I should say not! Bees just love lions' roars. It puts them to sleep even in the middle of the day."

Just then a swarm of bees lands on the tree.

BEAR: "Really? Say, how about coming around tomorrow morning and roaring around this honey tree?"

LION: "My purr is even more soothing. Come over here a little closer where you can hear it better."

The moral of this fable is:

1. Bears ought to stop thinking about bees when they see lions.
2. Check out the new man in the territory before you invite him to roar.
3. Bears who believe tall stories aren't safe even in their own territory.
4. To some people, confidence sounds the same as truth.
5. A soft voice can be more dangerous than a roar.

After you've heard your colleague's fable again, write nonstop 3 or 4 morals of your own. Read all these around the room.

Here are 3 more morals for "Bear and Lion":

- Let sleeping bees lie.
- Never bare yourself to the lion's purr.
- Beware of soothing words from a sharp-toothed mouth.

Ask your group to recall one or two aphorisms. Have them reread so that everyone can copy them.

The next step is to write briefly nonstop, and it's important to write for the whole time, even if your mind idles through one of your sentences. This is not a test. You can't do it wrong—except by waiting to write till you think of something impressive or important. If you're stuck, go back to the first thing you said and say something still more obvious.

Pick the aphorism that interests you most, and write for 3 minutes nonstop what you notice about how the sentence is written. For example, in the aphorism, "Bears ought to stop thinking about bees when they see lions," I notice the meaning isn't complete until the last word. Don't stop before the 3 minutes are up, and begin with the obvious.

Read all these observations aloud, listening to them as you would listen to a set of fables, without interrupting them for comment or discussion. You'll find surprises and recognitions among them, so don't miss hearing any of them, even those that apparently repeat. Repetitions, too, have something to tell you.

Here are some observations about the aphorism, "Bears ought to stop thinking about bees when they see lions.":

- The sentence includes all 3 characters from the fable.
- It gives the 3 characters some relation to each other.
- It centers around bears.
- I like it because it's so close to the terms of the fable.
- It remains nicely concrete, with bears, bees, lions.
- The sentence uses no adjectives.
- In the fable, the words *bear* and *lion* are singular. In the moral, the words are plural. So the moral says something about all bears and all lions.
- The word *thinking* suggests humans.
- All the words are everyday words.
- *Ought* suggests a detached point of view, neither for nor against bears or lions.
- The sentence doesn't give advice to the bear of the fable or to the reader. It speaks of bears in general.
- The sentence opposes *thinking* and *seeing*.

What do you learn from the pleasure of listening to a variety of beautiful sentences? The written sentence is the mirror of all longer writing. What the sentence does in its well-fitted frame, extended writing can do. And as you observe the sentence, you build a store of ideas for extended writing and a vocabulary for describing all other writing.

Put this way of paying attention and responding to writing into practice every time you meet. Listen to the author. Then recall something that attracted you in what you heard. If it's a single sentence, ask the author to reread it so you can copy it. If it's longer, make observations on what you remember most vividly. Write nonstop so that your writing flows unself-consciously out of the activity of attention. And begin with the obvious, which is the attractive center of your attention.

As you listen to the first observations your group writes, you notice the excitement of trying a form or technique for the first time. Newness sharpens perceptions. Catch these perceptions while they're fresh. After everyone in your group has read observations, write nonstop for 5 minutes to what you noticed about writing observations and listening to them. Read these to each other and hear them all without interruption.

Reread your own observations on each day's batch of writing. Write down the ones you've heard that mean the most to you. Then mark the best observations. Copy these into an *Observations* section of your writer's notebook.

When you have a page full of observations, read them over. Then write 2 or 3 sentences saying what these observations suggest about your own writing and the kind of writing your group is doing. When your group has finished a whole set of assignments, read some of these reflective sentences to each other.

8

Prolific Writing

You've seen, in the fable, one way to evoke the power of your language to uncover what you have in mind. It's the way of starting with a literary structure. Such a shape is a strong ally; you can count on it to draw good things from the inner world of language out onto the page. The structure itself calls forth what it needs to take on life. Often we write more than we knew we know. Structure has that power.

There's another way to draw on the power of language. It's different. In fact, it's the polar opposite of structured writing. It gets you writing spontaneously, recording your language in an unguided flow. That's the next thing you'll practice: prolific writing.

This writing is generous-minded. It's pure play, pure exploration, and can't be done wrong. It's active but relaxed, a way to collect and recollect your rich mental world.

Time yourself, and write for 10 minutes *without stopping*. Don't plan ahead, correct, pause to reflect, or try to organize your thoughts. Just start writing right away, and keep writing whatever comes. (Should you get stuck, write "the the the"; your mind will refuse to be bored and slip you a noun and more to go on with.)

Now, read your prolific writing to the group, and listen to the others read theirs.

Anything goes in prolific writing. It's a gamble of 10 minutes for which you'll always have something to show and some growth in invisible skill—and sometimes you'll hit the jackpot so that ideas and discoveries will pour onto the page, as good as gold.

Here's an important term-long, long-term assignment: Do 10 minutes of prolific writing each day for the rest of the semester. You'll have time to acquire a writing habit, and many chances to experiment. Try to find time every other week for your group to read some prolific writing aloud to each other. Among writers, the special good things are as catching as the common cold.

Choose a notebook especially for prolific writing. I like the sewn kind myself, because they keep well. They are not flimsy, and they feel like a book, my book.

Prolific writing is loose but efficient. It makes writing agreeably habitual. You can always find the crack in time, the odd 10 or 20 minutes, even in days too crowded to allow the luxury of leisurely composition. It's a surprise and a satisfaction to observe how much writing you get down in these short daily stints. You've already done something important, by taking time regularly, and regularly filling a page with words. You've made a decisive move toward forming the one habit—daily writing—a writer needs.

What can you do with all those pages? Whatever you like. See prolific writing as more than a diary or journal. It's part of your raw material as a writer. Sculptors have marble or clay; writers have notebooks stuffed with encouraging drafts of possibilities.

You can read it over and mark it with a different pen or pencil where you're struck by a promise in the flavor of the words or the fore-edge of an idea.

You can both read and write prolific writing for the random free enjoyment of the shaping power of language. All the years of your life have gone into gathering and nourishing your mind's verbal richness. Use prolific writing to reflect thought out of your mind and onto the saving page.

Try out ideas for papers you've been assigned, or letters you owe, or stories you want to record. Or just jump from phrase to phrase for fun, because you like the way they sound. Write, perhaps for longer periods, in the same nonstop way to find out what you really think about anything—your choice of a field of study, your dreams of bliss eternal or temporal, your new shoes and where you'll walk in them.

Here are two practical suggestions:

1. From now on, when you write, remind yourself that you expect lively things to emerge. That betters the odds at once. The preconscious life of language in the mind isn't directly accessible. But it is wonderfully suggestive. Tell yourself you want gemstones along with the ordinary diggings of thought, and be ready for anything. You know from hearing your colleagues read that there's no end to the voices—anecdotes, daydreams, gorgeous sounds, keen perceptions—that echo through language. As the first reader of what you write, expect yourself to be a writer whose work will reward close reading with unpredictable pleasure. You needn't expect what you'll write; just expect that you'll write, and that it will be good.

2. Begin by naming concrete objects and actions. Set down plain-as-day an active view of mental images. Try dialogue—a little play of words. Or tell the story of now to your future self, or recall what you saw as a child before you had the right words to express it, or praise what you love and mock what you despise in all their particulars.

It takes at least a dozen concrete sentences to earn one abstract sentence. The more concrete most of your words are, the more inventive your abstract words will be. To cure sluggish writing, trust what you can see to evoke what you can't see. Abstract ideas are the crown of concrete experience. The deep mixture of abstract and concrete is the genius of language; turning to the concrete is the gesture which summons that genius for us.

Naming feelings is, in comparison, a feeble way to hint at what you have felt. That's probably because language has as its first aim to name and relate the world of beings and events. Let language about the tangible outer world teach you to transport your inner world into writing. To get more of the surge and current of feeling into words, work with the primal language of acts and objects, and see where it takes you.

9

About Sentences

You've written, rewritten, and made observations about aphorisms. Now take another look at those good rewritten sentences, to consider their wholeness and the interaction of their parts.

Shift your point of view, from being their writer to being their reader, and focus on them from that short distance. What are they like?

Each of them is a sample of the essential literary structure, the sentence, that splendid human invention which is so close a necessity that we heed it as little as we do our heartbeat, so close a necessity that it's hard to measure or define.

You have been articulating such sentences ever since you left infancy, with the remarkable ability we call grammar-power.

Here's a little device, not a theoretical definition but a handy, practical recognition-guide, which you can use to identify the wholeness of your sentence structures: *in a complete sentence you can find an unsubordinated subject and its verb*. It may contain other parts of language, but it must have an unsubordinated subject and its main verb.

Look at your sentences from this point of view, and you'll discover that they sort out into three kinds. These classifications also appear in traditional grammar, where you may have met them already. Writers become aware of them because they present mental structures which are literary as well as grammatical. They show three kinds of order:

> There's *the order of simple assertion*, in a simple sentence with its unsubordinated subject and verb (for instance: "Birds fly." "Each bird is a world of infinite delight." "Cardinals and chickadees eat seeds.")

> There's *the order of coordination*, in a coordinated (or compound) sentence with two equally ordered assertions, each having its own unsubordinated subject and verb. (For instance: "Birds fly; snakes slither." "Bats and flycatchers eat insects, but cardinals and chickadees eat seeds.") Here there are two assertions in each whole structure, each *with* its own subject and verb and *without* a subordinating word before the subject. Each assertion could stand as a syntactically complete sentence on its own if the author chose.

There's *the order of subordination*, in a subordinated (or complex) sentence with two assertions ordered unequally: one of the assertions uses an unsubordinated subject and its verb, while the other assertion uses a subordinating word in front of (or as) the subject, which is followed by its verb. (For instance: "*Because* flycatchers eat insects, they ignore the feeder full of sunflower seeds." "*If* this isn't clear, don't worry." "*After* you've lived with it for a while, it will be more clear." "It's the mental gesture of subordination *which* I find interesting.") Note that the emphasized words are subordinators. Only the assertion without a subordinator could stand as a syntactically complete sentence on its own. (For instance: "Don't worry." "It will be more clear.")

See how many of your rewritten sentences you can sort out into one of these three classes. If a few don't fit, don't strain over them. Look at those which do fit. Notice how they work.

We don't pretend there are rules with the authority to govern your sentence-making. There are no such rules. No one would use them if there were. Nothing much would ever get said, for it would be no fun to crank such a machine.

Yet there are grammatically-named elements you can reflect on when you read, classify, or rewrite sentences. The wholeness of a sentence is part of its power. You sense that wholeness with your grammar-power, your knowledge of your mother-tongue (whether or not that be English). You can test for wholeness, if you wish, by referring to the recognition-guide. You can practice identifying sentences until you sense their mental shape as simple, coordinated, or subordinated. This is not a waste of time, for these are also mental shapes for essays.

10

The Parable

We all have hundreds of stories in our heads, though most of us aren't conscious of them. They may come to mind when we hear someone talk about grandma's car or an eccentric first-grade teacher. They are more than reports; they're about happenings that have taken root in memory because they're packed with meaning. Most of them are family stories we've heard or lived. The longer they have been remembered, the stronger the proof that they're worth remembering.

Older members of my family like to recall the gone world of their early days. Great-Aunt Minnie has always talked about her 8th-grade students in Brownsville; one story was about a boy who taught his parents their third language, English, by getting them to help with his homework. Bachelor Great-Uncle Tom would talk about going to the South Street docks in July to scrape delicious licorice, which had melted and seeped through the staves, from the outside of barrels it was shipped in. Then he'd show his knife, the same knife, and remark that most people don't hold onto things the way he did. Father still showed traces of the pride he'd felt then, as he described delivering bread and rolls at 5 AM, before school, and coming home to pour his wages on the kitchen table where his mother was preparing breakfast, the year his father died. Great-Uncle Van was the one for clothes stories—his first real suit, his woes with shoes for his big but narrow feet. Everyone would groan when he began, and I'd think, "Not that again!" but they were in fact stories that rang true to who he was and what he valued.

Take 20 minutes, and write nonstop in search of such stories. Look for stories you've heard from grandparents and other older people. You won't know ahead of time, possibly, what you'll find, but you're sure to come on something. If a memory presses to be told fully at once, do that. Or you may jot down, nonstop, quick phrases for later development. (Write, for example, "the story about the wrong jacket," "the story about the fall down stairs," "the story about the cesspool and the wedding.") We call them family parables because of the way they make domestic use of the ancient and noble parable structures in which the story turns around and makes a point that identifies the character.

Read your nonstop writing, and listen well to those of your colleagues. Hearing others' stories quickens recollection. When all have read, take another 10 minutes and write nonstop. Since many stories are about moments common to human lives—holidays or jobs, games or school-days, meetings that led to weddings or fatal accidents—one story recalls others. It's as if we have a place in our minds, a kind of walled garden where identifying anecdotes cluster; once we've found the gate in the wall, we can go back there more readily.

Take home your nonstop pages of notes and starts. Choose one story, and write it out.

Your next assignment will be to set down more of these stories. They're valuable. The older the story, the better it may sound. That's because memory keeps only the best parts, held in the best order, ready to retell.

For now, we don't ask you for stories of what happened to you recently; such writing is a bit more tedious. You'd have to decide which parts tell the most, find a center from which to order them, and pray to strike the right tone, neither vain nor sarcastic, neither a report nor a cliché. Luckily, what's stored in mind is plentiful; it's already edited and ordered for safekeeping by the invisible, intuitive muse of memory. Your mind has already done the work. And you can get at it through patient, rummaging, prolific writing.

Your power as a writer expands through capturing these stories which memory has shaped. For one thing, grasping and recording them gives you practice in using your mind as your greatest natural writer's resource. Poking around in the mental attic is a good beginning. No matter how abstruse or complex the subject, we can write only what we have in mind. All writing is getting something out of your head and onto a page.

11

Adjective → Noun → Paragraph

As usual, we take the next step forward by taking a brief look backward. Read a family parable aloud, one of your own or one by a colleague. Think about the most important character at the crucial moment of the story.

Write a short list of adjectives—say 4 to 6 of them—which describe the most important character's behavior as it makes a difference to the story. Read all the lists aloud.

Now you have in mind a sizable and varied collection of adjectives. (For instance: self-conscious, disappointed, worried, mindful, over-protected, conscientious, obedient, anxious, moralizing, old-fashioned, fated, thoughtful, responsible).

Read through the list and choose the adjective you think fits most neatly.

Turn that adjective into a noun. (For instance, choosing *worried* would give you WORRY; *lucky* would give LUCK; *conscientious* becomes CONSCIENTIOUSNESS; *anxious* becomes ANXIOUSNESS or ANXIETY; *mindful* becomes MINDFULNESS.)

Write a sentence beginning with that noun and followed by the verb *is*. Then complete the sentence. (For instance, "Mindfulness is paying heed to what you do and taking it to heart." "Conscientiousness is looking at the right and wrong of actions before and after leaping into them.")

Now, to fill out the definition that sentence gives, say more. Write a few more sentences to tell more about your idea of the noun. (For instance, "It weighs and balances what to do and what has been done. It's anxious to do the right thing. It does not depend on luck. It takes responsibility.")

You have just written a paragraph which defines an abstraction. You've gone step by step through a process you usually accomplish in a flash of intuition. You've pulled out of the story an idea of what it means to you. Practicing the steps consciously helps ready you to write at demand as well as at will.

Once again, read your work and listen to your colleagues read theirs; it will once again broaden and deepen your sense of what's possible. You may have second thoughts of what else you might say. Quickly rewrite your paragraph to include them.

This exercise bears repeating. Take another parable; reread it till you have some adjectives to fit its central character. Make a noun of one of them, and define the noun. Then write at least 4 or 5 more sentences which unpack the possibilities of definition by saying more about the abstract word.

Write paragraphs in this way for 4 or 5 of your family parables.

Here's something you might like to try when composing the few additional sentences. Look back at the original list of adjectives you've compiled and consider incorporating one or two of them— or nouns derived from them or other words which convey their quality—into your sentences. In the instance above, on conscientiousness, "anxious" and "responsibility" occur because the writer looked at the original list and found those ideas useful as she amplified her definition.

Practice this defining paragraph. It leads to a writer's skill that follows logically from the skills you've accumulated so far. Skills not only perfect themselves through use without being measured. They increase fastest when they build on and balance one another. Constructing this paragraph raises to consciousness your power to move from concrete to abstract language. It's practice in examining your concrete data and abstracting your idea from it. So long as you keep deepening your access to your own language by writing prolifically every day, this structural breakdown of the process of composition will increase your control without cutting into your fluency.

12

The Simple Essay

Now that you have a paragraph of abstract definition, here's how to use it.

Write it down as paragraph one of an essay.

Under it, write the family parable from which you derived the noun which begins paragraph one. The parable now becomes the concrete example you need as the middle part of an essay.

Read over what you now have. Write a concluding paragraph in which you return to the idea of paragraph one and express the difference the example makes to what you can say about the idea.

The result is a simple expository essay; that is, it is a piece of writing which supports the idea it asserts.

Paragraph one is abstract; it asserts and defines an idea.

The middle paragraphs are concrete; they present an example which supports the idea.

The concluding paragraph brings them together and offers a fuller view of the idea.

Each of your family stories can stand as an example in the middle part of an expository essay, in which the idea asserted is drawn from the concrete story.

You have been practicing the order of events natural to writing all exposition, however simple or scholarly. Here's another way to describe that order, which may be useful if you're writing papers on assigned subjects for other courses:

Begin with concrete expression—written nonstop, perhaps—of what you notice you have in mind, from reading or experience, on your chosen subject. This is your raw material.

Discover an idea generated by considering what you have expressed concretely. Write down that idea. (It may be called your hypothesis.) It's the rough draft of your first paragraph.

Return to the concrete you've already expressed and to the observation and exploration of what you have concretely in mind. Use the idea, or hypothesis, to select from all you know those parts of concrete evidence, or demonstration, which best come together to support your idea. (This support might, in some cases, be called proof, though most real ideas are not strictly provable.)

Arrange those parts. They're the rough draft of the middle of your essay.

Draw a concluding statement from what they show about your idea. You will need 4 or 5 good sentences. (This might be called your thesis, which has by now been demonstrated.) This is the rough draft of your end paragraph.

You can see that family stories are one instance of the many thought-provoking things you know and can use to explain an idea in the middle paragraphs of an expository essay. Anything you know about well enough to think about and find ideas is potential material for the middle of an essay.

This exercise opens out for your inspection a view of the mental path which discourse may take to arrive at an expository essay. The mind has the power to generate ideas about what it knows; it's something we all can do, do often, and do differently.

This way is just one reliable way among many. It has the advantage of being repeatable and therefore useful to us who want to practice. You can count on it to get you started on any subject you know, since it calls on the energy of thought as it moves dynamically between concrete and abstract. The bond between your idea and your evidence will be not only strong, as it should always be, but it will also be obvious, which gives you—without trying—real practice in awareness of how concrete evidence and abstract idea interact.

You'll see, as you read the family stories you've used as the heart of essays, how the concrete narrative has called out the abstract definition and made it substantial. At the same time, the abstract broadens the reach and use of the story by defining what you understand it to mean. Discovering your view of the idea that makes your story worth telling, and describing the significance you've discovered, opens storytelling to a larger view in a new dimension, the literary dimension of expository essays. Your narrative has become a demonstration, with no loss to its original sense. You are informing your readers on the two levels of abstract and concrete, which evoke, shape, and complete each other.

Keep practicing this essay shape until you've turned each of your family parables into an expository essay.

Just for fun and for more practice, you might try the shape with 2 or 3 of your fables, by experimenting with the most abstract of your aphorisms as the central sentence of the first paragraph. Write the first paragraph to include a definition of the key idea of the aphorism, and develop it in a few more abstract sentences. Copy out your fable as the middle paragraphs of an essay demonstrating concretely what the first paragraph says. Read it all through, and compose a conclusion.

13

Reading Aloud, Listening, Writing Observations

There's a fair and simple way of "publishing"—making public—all the essays your group writes. Bring them to your meeting and read them aloud to each other. Begin at one end of the room and read right around. Don't ask for volunteers; you want the fact of reading to be comfortable so that the fun of listening will be illuminating.

If you run into a difficulty like foreign accents or a speech impediment, pay no attention to it. It's no problem. Keep reading; keep listening, and in a few meetings you won't hear the difficulty any more—only the good writing. No one else can have your voice for your writing, so it's important to read your own work.

After each essay is read, take one minute and write nonstop what you noticed about how the essay is written, just as you wrote observations on your aphorisms (Chapter 7). Describe the way the essay is written and designed; begin with the obvious. Don't write opinions or evaluations. Hold on to the observations, but don't read them yet.

When all the essays have been read, read your observations aloud to the authors. You'll hear some remarkable observations. Listen to them with expressions of interest, but don't interrupt them.

Here's an essay (though not a "Simple Essay") with three sets of observations to give you a sense of how they work. Begin by reading the essay aloud.

ONCE I WAS...NOW I AM

Once I was a student at Rutgers University, but now I am a student at Queens College. Big deal, big difference, one might think, just the transfer from one school to another. But there is a big difference, six years of difference, six years of independence, of earning my own living, of learning the hard way, of two-bit jobs, of getting nowhere. Six years ago I was a grass-green country boy from the rolling hills of Hunterdon County,

New Jersey's most rural county. I was going to college because I had no car to get to a job, and rural Hunterdon had no public transportation. I had a 4-F medical draft deferment, and therefore the army as an option was unavailable to me. I was an engineering major, not because I was interested, but because I had done well in math and science in high school.

I was not ready for college and after one year I left and moved to New York City. Suddenly gone were money from home, a dormitory and meals cooked for me. I had to get a job. I did, and in the past six years I have worked as a messenger, mail clerk, dishwasher, and waiter among other jobs, never earning more than $3.25 an hour and sometimes working 12 to 16 hours a day to make ends meet. I had to find a place to live. I did, in a rapidly deteriorating section of the Bronx, roaches and rats free of charge, but on my wages I couldn't afford a penthouse suite. I had to buy and prepare my own meals. I did; grits, mush, chicken backs and necks, potatoes and lard fit the bill because I could afford them. There had to be a better way.

Though New York City had the convenience of a mass transit system, the medical facilities necessary to monitor the condition that resulted in my 4-F draft classification, in addition to stores, parks and other city features, I never planned to live here. I wasn't comfortable in a city. But last year I worked at a job in Flushing, Queens. I could afford it and to avoid a two-hour subway ride to the Bronx at 3 AM when I finished work, I moved to Flushing. Flushing is in Queens and therefore part of the city of New York, but compared to the Bronx it was like home. I could live in Flushing with peace of mind. With my mind free of thoughts of "getting out" I could think about the future, about the better way.

The future I chose after six years away from guidance counselors, teachers and parents was dietetics. The condition with which I am afflicted requires, among other things, that I ingest a low copper diet. (Copper is a trace mineral in foods.) It was this requirement that aroused my interest in the field of dietetics.

Once I was a student at Rutgers University; now I am a student at Queens College. Once somebody else chose my future; now I am choosing my future. Once I was six long years younger than I am now.

*   *   *

Examples of Observations

A. I like the eloquent follow-up to the parallel structure of the first sentence: *of . . . , of . . . , of. . . .* The parallels carry him through the *first* past of the essay: *I had to . . . I did,* several times. Then the salting of negatives stops, and he asserts the present in a way which ties it back to the past *before* the essay. The core of the essay is choice: first others choosing for you: Rutgers, engineering, leaving Rutgers; then choosing change within New York City, choosing a field of study. The choice is credible, gradual, and blessed with luck as he comes closer to himself in choosing a present which is rooted and is looking at the future. There are telling and well-limited personal details (low copper diet). The pick-up, at the end, of the initial sentence shows how far he has come in six years and how far he has brought us in a few minutes. It lifts the essay in the direction of idea, of a philosophy, because it includes a perception the writer presents of his own life as a whole life.

B. "Six years" appears at least three times, roughly at beginning, middle, and end.

The first part of the essay might be called the "negative." That begins almost immediately with "big deal" and "big difference."

The "wandering" or unhappiness begins to end with "There had to be a better way." The phrase "better way" is, like the "six years," repeated.

The essay has in it nothing that it doesn't *use,* and much of it comes up again—the illness that made him 4-F, for example.

The writer makes it very clear that the change he's describing comes with maturity, and is a change from doing what others wanted him to do to what *he* chose to do.

The essay is not exactly packed with concrete details, but they're there—in his poverty diet of hominy grits and so on, for example. And dietetics turns out to be the subject of study he chooses for *himself.*

The change from Rutgers to Queens College is a change from country to city which passes through the Bronx as a way-station. This middle term makes part of the "negative" experience or the wandering. And it's a more extreme difference from home than Flushing is/was.

He makes it plain that he began college—at Rutgers—because there was very little else he could do. He had no choice, or very little. He ends by really choosing.

The time between—the six years—have prepared and influenced the choice, but not forced it.

Perhaps we could say that he sees his affliction finally as offering him an opportunity—giving him a subject of study.

C. The writer barely mentions his disease at first. It comes up by the way or in subordination to some other point. His "condition" moves from the periphery of the story to the center.

The most important hope (called "the future," "the better way") then comes out of this very condition or disease.

It's as if something formerly pushed aside or avoided or thought about in a language (*deferment, ingest, trace mineral*) separate from the writer's ordinary language—as if that turned out to belong to the center, and when it was placed in the center, it produced fruit.

"Better way" is mentioned twice. The second time it's associated with "the future."

The essay is mostly a narrative of the time *between* the *once* and the *now* of the first sentence. It doesn't seem to have two parts but to be a narrative between two parts.

But the essay does have sets of strong, two-part contrasts: Hunterdon/Bronx, Bronx/Flushing, others choosing for you/self choosing.

These contrasts are what he thinks about or realizes in the time of *in between* of his essay.

The unpleasantness of the city didn't make him want to return to the country. It doesn't turn him back, but ahead, toward "the future."

The future seems to be something beyond both the country and the Bronx.

Concrete language about food—the only detailed concrete language of the essay. It foretells the writer's professional interest in diet.

*   *   *

Check what are for you the most interesting of these observations and write quickly what you liked about them. For example, I noticed that each set is very different and yet they all agree.

14

Rewriting: Endings

By now you've written and read aloud a few simple essays, listened to colleagues read theirs, and written and read your observations.

This practice in producing and appreciating the elemental whole structure of exposition has developed your skill at sensing the whole and its basic parts. It's important to begin, as you have, by focusing on the shape of the whole. One result is that you can sense the impulse of each part toward enhancing the overall structure.

Here's a way to rewrite which will tell you more about the whole structure as it is affected by the ending.

Bring your next assigned simple essay to class with the last paragraph written on a separate sheet of paper.

In class, listen while one of your group reads an essay up to but not including the last paragraph. Write and read observations on the beginning and middle. Have the two parts read again, still omitting the ending.

Write, in some 5 to 10 sentences, a fitting ending for the idea and its support which you have just heard.

Read these thoughts around the room.

And do it again: listen to another simple essay, without its ending; write and read observations, hear the reader again, then compose another last paragraph that, by showing how the middle part has developed the beginning, brings the whole to a conclusion.

Read these aloud, too.

Before you leave this session, exchange the beginning and middle of your assigned essay with a colleague. (Hold on to the sheet of paper containing the ending you have written.) As homework, read the parts you have of your colleague's essay. Quickly write as many observations as you can. Go back, read the parts over, and write more observations, till you have plenty of them. Read your observations over and compose a paragraph that concludes your colleague's structure.

During the next meeting, give the whole essay to your colleague, and when you've received your own, take it home to read from beginning through ending.

This exercise is intriguing.

It asks the reader for accuracy and purposeful attention. It's also a real test. It tests how readily intelligible the beginning and middle paragraphs are. As you read your colleague's new conclusion for your idea and its support, you'll have a good concrete sample of how a reader perceives them. It will be full of implications about your essay. It can tell you a lot. It may suggest changes—perhaps in idea or emphasis or data—which you can make to strengthen your first and middle paragraphs.

It also tells you of the job a concluding paragraph does: it brings out the insight to which your idea and its support lead the reader. You'll see that, if the beginning assertion of the idea is definite and the middle support is concrete and in good order, a good reader can compose an en ing that fits. It may be different from the one the author wrote, but it too will fit.

Once the first two parts are in place, the conclusion follows from them. That's what this exercise tests. Since the test is direct (and self-scored), it also teaches. It reminds us that a conclusion is the next natural thing to say, after we say our idea and the evidence we have for it: X is what I think: Y is what I know about it; I therefore conclude XYZ—the three big parts of an expository essay.

It incidentally makes clear that you can't deduce someone else's first or middle paragraphs from any 2 other parts. You can't have someone else's voice or idea. You can't write out the supporting data from which their idea sprang, since that too is in the mind of the writer.

But you can draw a conclusion, from what the writer has given you. That's the function of an ending. Yours won't read the way the original writer's does. But it will do the same thing: state the implications of the idea as the support has developed it. From the two first parts, the last part follows. You can always rewrite the end of your papers, any papers, by rereading the beginning and middle, and saying what follows from them.

Try it, by reading the first two parts of one or two of your earlier simple essays, making observations and writing new last paragraphs. The better the essay, the more it will profit from—and the likelier it is to bring forth—a really fine conclusion. Remember this way of rewriting the end after rereading the first parts. It's always a good way to test the intelligibility of your idea and the coherence of its support.

Once you're satisfied with the way your ending follows from the rest, here's another step to take:

Read over your last sentence—or perhaps your last 2 sentences. (Rereading is the first business-like step toward rewriting.) Then, recalling the way you've rewritten aphorisms, rewrite what the sentences say, perhaps in new language, perhaps using some of the same expressions. This time you're working for the aphoristic qualities of elegance and memorability. Work on them to give them the power of a concluding rhythm. Let them sound like what they are: the ultimate assertion of the essay's reason for being.

This rewriting to find the strongest form of your conclusion should be done for every piece of writing. We all know quite a bit about having a last word, the way the aphorism does in a fable. A conclusion gives you a chance to bring it all home. Make it a habit to rewrite the last sentence, till it is self-evident and memorable because it is quintessential.

15

Pronouns

Extending what you know you know, as you do in rewriting, is the elegant way to acquire skill. You can see learning as starting with a base camp, where you're sure of how to operate, which you expand by advancing from it and returning to advance further.

Here's another excursion to try. It takes you through an area you know so well you take it for granted. Advancing to bring that knowledge under conscious control will keep your essays fluent and free of error or confusion.

Notice that, when you write, you—perhaps indirectly or unconsciously—give the reader essential information about who, in this writing, is the speaker of the piece. Your sentences use pronouns (or nouns that can be switched to pronouns) in the first, second, or third person: in the singular, I, you, he, she, it, one; in the plural, we, you, they.

The pronoun guides your imagination, by fixing the point of view from which you imagine the language of your essay. It guides the reader, by identifying the voice of the speaker. It acts to integrate the essay; it runs like a scarlet thread throughout, clarifying the whole structure.

Essays for which you choose the pronoun with care will be more clear and wonderfully liberated from the tangles of confused pronoun reference. You—and so, your readers—can then imagine the essay consistently, seen through the eyes of that speaker, from that pronoun's point of view.

To establish your use of points of view, begin by thinking of books, papers, lectures, conversations you've read and written.

Write down the word "I"; then turn out a good 8 minutes of nonstop prolific writing on "I." What are its strong points? What do you use it for? When? To whom do you use it? What do you think it does best? How do you like the way others use it?

Don't be afraid to half-repeat yourself, and don't skimp. Be lavish in pointing out more and more of what your experience of the written and spoken "I" has told you. Especially feel free to include the obvious. (You're making observations. This time you're observing not a piece of writing, but the contents of your mind, gathered from all your experience with language.)

Do the same for the other 8 pronouns. (You can't do it wrong.)

When you've laid it all out, you'll have the beginnings of a survey of pronouns that govern voices you can use when you write. You probably already have a favorite pronoun for essays. Think about how it serves you and about practicing with other, less familiar, governing pronouns as a way of expanding your working lines of thought.

(By *governing*, we mean the writer has parcelled out, to the pronoun, some of the work of unifying the essay. Consistent verb tenses also aid in governance, and the great governor is the writer's idea. Writers achieve governance, or coherence, by thoroughly imagining the time and speaker of the essay and what the speaker is talking about.)

You'll need to hear your colleagues' explorations, too. Add to your own notes those of their thoughts which make sense to you.

Take these notes, and rework them into lists, 9 of them, one for each of the possible alternatives. You'll need 9 sheets of paper for this task. Leave space at the bottom to add ideas as they occur to you in the course of writing essays and papers from now on.

You may find the lists fall into parallel with each other, point for point. Or you may like to make charts; if so, you can produce one. It will be like a cognitive map for all 9 governing pronouns.

The choice, every time you begin a piece of writing, is yours. All 9 have useful functions. (We think it's a good notion to avoid "one" because it generates mistakes in reference—but that's just a warning.) Choosing the one that best fits your idea and development—and sticking to it wherever suitable—gives your work the strength of continuity. It will reach your readers and let them hear the voice you think appropriate.

From now on, make it a first step in writing essays: decide on a governing pronoun.

16

Rewriting: Beginnings

You've considered whole structures, sentences, observations, grammar, pronouns, and their powers—all in behalf of your essays.

You've practiced rewriting the most public part of an essay, the final paragraph, which publishes the conclusion you draw from your idea and its support.

Now consider beginnings. A first paragraph is an original definition. It puts forth your idea about the concrete information of the middle paragraphs.

You want it as definite as you can get it—even more for your own sake than for the reader. The clearer your stated idea, the more help it gives you in finding the best order for the data, when you rewrite your middle paragraphs.

Abstract beginning and concrete middle are interdependent; each explains, or exposes, the other in its own way. Often, you'll compose the beginning *after* you've written a rough draft of the middle. Then, in rewriting the middle, you'll use paragraph one as a Geiger counter to detect, among the data you've assembled there, which parts are most active and fit.

The beginning also—and at the same time—introduces and identifies the you who is the speaker of the essay. It incorporates your choice of a stance, a point of view, a voice and persona. The first paragraph, stating your idea, is personal to you and sets the tone which governs the whole essay.

Establish a firmly consistent speaker's point of view by choosing your governing pronoun before you start. Hold it in mind throughout. By defining your stance as speaker, it keeps you imagining thoroughly what you, that speaker, are saying. Clarity, unity, coherence are words for qualities we can't point to but like to hear about our writing. They indicate, in effect, readers' pleasure when a writer has thoroughly imagined a whole essay. Trust a governing pronoun to clue them in. Whenever you complete a whole first draft, reread it to make sure one person is saying the sentences (save for direct quotations, of course) right from the start.

You'll also want to rewrite your beginning at the level of the sentence, as you did for aphorisms and final sentences. This kind of rewriting, for which you've already developed some skill, is always fruitful.

Choose one of your simple essays, and write at least 5 versions of its very first sentence. Recopy the one you like best, and compose a few sentences which flow from it to round out the definition of your idea. Read it, and read your original first paragraph again. Then rewrite a third paragraph—the first rewrites may both have features you want to keep. Work to introduce your idea worthily, using the voice you want to govern your whole essay.

Because the idea and the point-of-view are original and uniquely under the author's authority, authors stand responsible for the statement of the first paragraph. Rewrite it, knowing you can try and toss out as many versions as you like till you get one which you are willing to honor. That's a lot quicker and calmer than believing you have to get it perfectly right in one try.

A curious fact about beginnings: they're not the easiest part of an essay to rewrite, yet they're often the part you spontaneously want to work on. During the time it takes to compose the draft of an essay, you'll often come on a new idea about the material. Sometimes this discovery comes at the last minute, in the extra time you take to write or type a clean copy. The new idea may be more speculative, or more complete, or more true to the data. It can charge the subject with excitement so sharp you'll talk to yourself and say things like, "That's it; yes; so that's what it means; that's what I meant; that's the idea."

Such a high creative moment of new vision is the writer's reward for writing. No one can demand or guarantee it.

But rewriting—especially rewriting language you've already rewritten—is the best way to invite it. The habitual rewriter is in a position to expect it. It goes beyond rewriting, taking it to a greater coherence or insight.

This offshoot of rewriting we call revision.

In revision, the imagination makes an unpredicted leap to integrate the writer's mind. Though we can't ever be sure a fresh vision will strike us, we know that original ideas often have their origin in the act of rewriting. A persevering working attention to the words on the page makes more likely that moment of truth when you catch the flash of a second sight, a revision, of meaning.

Revision is extremely energizing. It calls up more than enough writing energy to carry you through writing the essay over, in its fresh light.

Here's another fringe benefit, another way to look at rewriting: words you have rewritten and revised, you have taken deeply into your mind. If you want really to learn something, write and rewrite about it until you envision it, and then write out what you see. Such an essay will last in memory, as itself and as a kernel of the latent mental energy which confirms us in the use and power of our writing.

17

Rewriting: The Middle of the Essay

An organized essay has parts that work easily, organically, as if from within, to enliven each other and the whole. The big, fundamental parts you've been practicing—beginning, middle, end—automatically constitute a shape. They articulate each other and the whole into an essay of exposition: your idea, your data, and the meaning of these.

There's intellectual *completeness* in the span between abstract beginning and concrete middle, a span reflected in the end.

There's intellectual *contemplation* in the full first-paragraph expression of your governing idea.

There's intellectual *action* in the consistency of the governing pronoun which speaks for you throughout.

Idea and voicing pronoun enhance each other. Each is like a bodily system—a nervous or circulatory system, perhaps. They work together to flesh out the essay's skeletal whole structure with an effective life of its own.

This imitation of life is organization—not a grid imposed from without, but an imagined understanding. It makes the essay more like a living organism, to which all the parts belong and contribute. It isn't part flea, part rock, part hot air, held together in a compartmented briefcase. It's organized from within during writing and rewriting. One of the aims of all rewriting is to enrich the vital interplay of parts. No matter how various the content, how surprising the idea, it all coheres as if it had a life of its own on the page, even in the absence of the author who imagined and composed it.

You've practiced rewriting ends and beginnings of whole essays, to express your ideas and emphasize your discoveries. The middle is the next part to consider.

Of course, every sentence in it can be rewritten as often as you like until it's lively and telling. By now you know how to oil the workings of your mind by rewriting at the level of the sentence. So we take for granted you'll be doing that.

In rewriting the entire middle part, the aim is to affirm the governance of your idea. Do this by going back to the core of data which inspired it, and giving the data a good display. Most useful notions about rewriting the middle will come to you while you are rereading it with slow attention. So the first step, to be repeated several times, is to reread.

Here are a few hints for rereaders who want a middle that is firm and serviceable to the whole:

1. The middle is at the service of the idea. At first, its concreteness inspired the idea. Now, as you reread to rewrite, look for the value of the data to the idea. Use that as your clue to arranging data. Let service to the idea organize the middle: go back and read paragraph one over again before reading each middle paragraph. Do one complete rereading this way. You may find sentences you can omit because they do nothing to support the idea. You may find an aspect of the idea for which no support yet appears; write it and include it where it belongs.

2. Notice the governing tense of the verbs. You've chosen it, rightly, with the intuitive rightness of your grammar-power. You've used that grammar-power to shift the verbs, where appropriate, from present to pluperfect or past or future, and back again. Still, it pays to make sure that, say in describing past events, you haven't slipped enthusiastically into a present tense without meaning to. Remember that a verb does more than stand for what a subject is doing or being. It tells what time it is. It can move in and around the time-line it establishes in your essay, giving it clock-and-calendar coherence.

3. Keep an eye out for ways to say more, more concretely (not just in more words) in answer to imaginary questions about your idea. Such questions sometimes remind you of data you want to add. The middle can give you answers to imaginary questions someone might pose after hearing your idea: "What makes you think so?" "Where did you get that idea?" "Oh yeah? Prove it!" "Sounds good, but exactly what do you mean?" "Can you tell me more about it?" In rereading, recall questions your first paragraph might provoke, and see if your middle paragraphs answer them.

4. Notice the concrete elements in each paragraph. Rewrite opaque sentences in which you've used generalities or clichés. ("Many of the media frequently utilize . . . "; "These days, in the modern lifestyle of our society . . . ") Throw them out, but gratefully, for they call your attention to a chance to unpack what you really mean, by crossing them out and imagining your point more thoroughly. Aim to leave no paragraph without the instant recognizability of the concrete.

5. If your data is in several parts which you need to separate and put in the most supportive order, you may sometimes find it

useful to stick signal-flags at the beginning of the paragraph. (You can sometimes take them out of the final draft, once writing has made the parts of your thinking clear to you.) Flag what the paragraph is for: "That's how it happened; now I'm going to say why"; "Here are three examples of how it used to be"; "This is the most evident case I know."

Reread your favorite essay, adding these hints to your sense of the organic and functioning whole. Then rewrite the middle of the essay.

Having worked as a rewriter at the level of the sentence and at the level of the whole essay, you'll never again make the mistake of thinking that when someone says, or writes in the margin, "Rewrite this," all you're allowed to do is correct the commas. You know what all real writers know: the joy and rewards of rewriting.

18

About Grammar

Grammar falls quietly and even beautifully into place, once we know what it is.

Yet if asked to define grammar, most of us would shrink from the task. Those who know names and rules for gerunds and gerundives and deep structures are usually just as confused as those who avoid writing because they dread fragments and run-on sentences. It takes very patient thinking to sort it all out. We want you to think along with us patiently, while we say some of our thoughts. They are more entertaining than they look, for they're useful and cheerful.

Grammar-Power

Perhaps the most punishing confusion comes from failure to separate grammar and grammar-power. Since grammar-power, the power to generate language, is vast, ancient, universal, delightful, and essential to writers—while grammatical systems are limited, recent, local, delightful, but not essential to writers—we'll talk first about grammar-power.

Grammar-power is a phrase we've found to name an identifying human capacity we recognize in ourselves and others. Grammar-power begins to develop in us as we learn to speak our mother tongue. It grows from the concrete, phrase-by-phrase, word-by-word experience of the infant and baby learning to listen and to speak, with effect, pleasure, and understanding.

We increase in grammar-power all our lives, as we speak, read, write, and listen, and as we realize experiences we strive to find language for. By now your grammar-power tells you at lightning speed how to write and speak sentences dense with meaning, your meaning, your sentences. You invent hundreds a day that you say aloud. Many more course through your mind carrying what you want to tell yourself.

Grammar-power, in all who speak a language, produces the concrete speaking and writing from which systems—and subsequent rules—of grammar have been abstracted. This is why your grammar-power and the rules of a grammar usually coincide.

It's why millions have spoken and written usefully and splendidly without systems or rules of grammar—often in languages never subjected to systematic analysis.

So the first move away from confusion about grammar is to assert and enjoy the grammar-power you unquestionably have. You've begun that by doing the work this book asks for, so far.

Here's an amazing fact: when you write and rewrite to capture the best, strongest, most telling sentences you can imagine, you are usually correct, too, as a secondary fringe benefit. *The wish to write well does more for correctness than the wish to be merely correct can do.*

That's not just because correctness is, indeed, elegant. It's because the comeliness of the body of the sentence depends on the health of its shapely inner structure. It's because the aim of writing well directs your trust in your own grammar-power. It puts attention where it belongs—on using your ability. Language presents meaning inseparable from structure; that is its property or characteristic quality. When you direct your grammar-power at fine sentences, rich in meaning, your mind intuitively produces sturdy structures. For what the mind generates is order, and the orderly structuring of language is likely to be as correct as it is handsome.

Hey, Wait

"But," someone says, "lots of people tell me I'm always making grammatical errors. How come?"

If some such question is in your mind, talk of grammar-power may make you restless. Patience! To relax with the grammar writers need, begin by prizing properly the grammar-power you already have, which is a home to you more intimate than your own skin.

Graphics

Now let's consider a major kind of error, frequently marked and fretted over, that is not grammatical, though often miscalled so. (Giving it the wrong name makes it harder to correct.) It is rightly named error in graphics—failure to follow the conventions of appearance in typed or written language.

Graphics include standardized spelling and marks of punctuation. Readers and writers honor them for the convenience of easier reading. Though very useful—and though reading much print leads us to expect them—they are not part of your grammar-power. You did not learn them when you learned your mother tongue. Note that when you read your work aloud, no one but you can tell anything about the graphics. Errors in graphics are not substantial; they evaporate in air.

Because good graphics open your work to easier reading in your absence, you want to use the code of graphics that gives unknown readers traces of your live voice. It's learned and practiced best while you're practicing reading and writing for their own sake. As your awareness of grammar-power grows, you'll turn at will to the conventions of punctuation which help you express yourself.

Here are the marks of punctuation we expect you'll practice in the writing we propose:

1. Begin the sentence with a capital letter.
2. End it with a period. (This or any page abounds in examples of these first two graphic marks.)
3. When a sentence contains more than one independent clause, join the clauses either
   a. by a semicolon (Roses are red; violets are blue.) or
   b. by a comma plus a conjunction (Honey is sweet, and so are you.)

You notice that all four of these graphic marks tell readers something about sentences. The sentence is the elemental whole structure, the vital carrier of thought. So marking off sentences is important to writers and their readers. These four marks show that the writer has identified the sentences so the reader can recognize them too.

Though commas have a dozen lesser uses, we call the comma before a coordinating conjunction THE comma in American English. Alone among commas, it announces a fact about the sentence as a whole. It says that the syntactic weight (of unsubordinated subject and its main verb) is the same on either side of the comma + conjunction. Master THE comma. Let other less potent uses of commas recommend themselves to you as you need them.

For graphics can be neat and helpful. As you go on writing, reading, listening, and observing, you'll recognize more of the constituent forms your grammar-power produces, and acquire more graphic signals.

Now is a good time to pick up a paper you've written and go through it with a pencil. Mark the times you've used each of the four graphic marks above. Visualize what one of your paragraphs would look like if you hadn't used any marks to ease the reading.

Notice the paragraphs in your paper, too. Paragraphs are another aid writers can give readers. Indenting the first of a group of sentences freshens the reader's eye for what your prose is up to. See how your paragraphs mark the stages of your thought for the reader. Recall how deadly a 3-page-long paragraph can look.

Paragraphing is even younger in the history of language and literature than grammar. It lies outside the words, outside the syntax. (Its name says it's a "beside-mark.") There are no rules for correct paragraphing. Take advantage of its flexibility to point out, for readers, your sense of your essay's whole structure. Step by step, paragraph by paragraph, bring the reader into the rhythm of your idea.

A sense of your own grammar-power and an eye attentive to the conventions of graphics will enable you to write well and correctly. Yet there's no reason to recoil from examining the categories of grammar. Here's a brief look at how they operate:

What Grammar Is

A grammar is a set of abstract statements about a language, drawn from many spoken and written examples of that language. Note that the grammar does not determine the language. Rather, the language, which is already alive and flourishing, supplies the basis of what the set contains, and so determines the grammar. The language, in the verbal acts of its speakers and writers, comes first, both in the personal experience of every writer and—by thousands of years—in the history of humanity.

Kinds

A grammar may be historical, telling how and generally why a language has changed over the centuries.

A grammar may be descriptive, assigning and describing general categories for all the events of a language—its words, and how they interact.

Or a grammar may be normative. It may, having described the events of a language, say that writers and speakers should now use the language according to a set of rules the grammarian has derived from the description. In other words, normative grammarians tell us we must do what they see we have been doing all along. Norms or rules tell us what the grammarian has found normal for our language, and what ways of using it will theoretically keep us able to understand each other. In practice, these normative overall guidelines may hold good for long periods, though languages with living speakers never stop changing in their particulars.

No one grammar has unique or absolute or eternal validity. A language may be analyzed into many historical grammars, many descriptive grammars, many normative grammars. This is possible because, as you know, from anything concrete—as language is—many different abstractions may legitimately be drawn.

It is normative grammar that most schools teach as an adjunct to writing courses. In this book, when we mention matters of grammar, we use the names and terms of a normative grammar, usually called "traditional" because traditional grammar is the kind most frequently used in business, in publication, and in handbooks of composition today.

Parts

Grammars usually distinguish 3 aspects of written language:

lexicon or dictionary: what it is that speakers use each word to name;

inflection: which words change, when and how they change, according to the way speakers use them (for instance: quick, quicker, quickest; I laugh, he laughed, she laughs.);

syntax: which words speakers put together, and in what order they arrange them, to express meaning—especially, how words work together in a sentence, the heart of the language.

Into these divisions, the ways you speak and write can be grammatically classified:

When you wrote aphorisms, some of you added a new word, *aphorism*, to your vocabulary. Your vocabulary is that part of the lexicon, or dictionary, which you have at your disposal.

When we suggest in Chapter 9 that you can identify the elements of a complete independent clause, or sentence, by looking for an unsubordinated subject and its main verb, we're talking about the interaction of subject and verb—a matter of syntax.

When you considered pronouns in Chapter 15, you thought about them as part of the lexicon (what you use them to stand for, or mean) and as elements of syntax (the way they interact with other words as you put them in place) and also as shapers of a speaker's rhetorical voice.

When you look to see that your verbs are consistent with one another and governed by the tense you've chosen, you consider the effects of inflection (the changes in the form of the verbs). In English, the most important inflection takes place in the way we form our verbs. Verbs are a particular glory of English; we can be wonderfully diverse and accurate in making them carry out our ideas.

(Here, just for fun, are samples of the variety possible in just the first-person singular verb form, showing only times passed: I was liking, I used to like, I did like, I have liked, I liked, I may have liked, I might have liked, I should have liked, I could have liked, I would have liked, I had liked, would I had liked.)

Luckily for us, the grammar-power we acquire before we're six gives us the elements of language in good working order. That includes inflection.

Some dialects inflect a few words in special ways. Those of you whose mother-tongues show some differences from the forms of normative grammar may want to enlarge your grammar-power to include the norms. It's a wise practical choice, though any shift in grammar-power takes time and care. You'll need to be patient and steady.

The commonest difference is in verbs. It's tiny. It's a change in 2—at most 4—bits of language, letters which show inflection. They are:

> the *s* or *es* ending of verbs in the 3rd person singular of the present tense (she paints; he walks; it seems) and the *d* or *ed* ending of regular past participles (painted; walked; seemed).

It's easy to memorize what the norm is. But that's the bare beginning. Internalizing the change can't be taught. Yet it can be learned, that is, self-taught. First and last, keep up plenty of practice in writing by trusting all the rest of the grammar-power you have. In 6–12 months of self-editing, the change will come fairly consistently into your spoken and written language. It's usually worth the trouble, since people often make wrong, mistaken, and insulting evaluations of those who don't follow this bit of the norm.

Grammar and This Book

You can see that this book gives you not grammar but the elements of writing. It identifies and names—sometimes in grammatical terms—the elements of language a writer can profit from practicing with conscious control. The elements for writers are those which do better than correct error; they help prevent it.

We want you to be a writer who is conspicuously ready, willing, and able. Research as well as experience and common sense shows that knowing grammar rules and scoring high on grammar exercises do not make people write better. In fact, rules and exercises, even when perfectly learned, produce among native speakers less than 10% improvement, even in mere correctness; the effort they entail is, as far as writing goes, 90% wasted.*

Plenty of writing, reading, and listening, however, are not wasted. They bring out more of what you can do, and lead you to

*Research spanning 60 years tells us this. It is summarized by George Hillocks in his 1983 synthesis of 72 earlier studies: "The study of traditional grammar has no effect on raising the quality of student writing."

do it better, more readily, and more correctly, all the time. We want this book to show you how and where a writer can use a system of grammar firmly subordinated to the real work, which is writing. We give you writers' priorities. They are: handsome sentences, a governing pronoun, a governing tense, a governing idea. Time spent on the work of writing well reinforces these grammatically-named aspects of grammar-power while you work.

The notion that you can't write well—and correctly—unless you've learned rules of grammar is a mistake, a spoiler of the pleasure natural to writers, and a spur to anxious confusion about grammar.

Uses

Then are we saying grammar is useless except to grammarians? No, never; though we do say that what's essential is what you have, grammar-power. It doesn't take much thought to realize that before we knew grammar of any kind, we had a basic, built-in supply of language, including matters of lexicon, inflection, and syntax, though it never occurred to us to notice or name them. We had the grammar-power writers can't do without. With grammar-power sharpened by abundant and observant writing, you can become a good and a correct writer without studying grammar abstractly.

But the more your sense of your own life excites you, and the more writing/reading/observing you do, the more you want to know about what language does for you, and how. You and your colleagues have begun taking advantage of your grammar-power by your close work and play with sentences. Writing and rewriting all shapes and kinds of sentences, and looking at plenty of good ones, is a fine place for writers to start. Then, giving grammatical names to the structures of your sentences expands your conscious control over your writing options. The sentence is your true first step because from it all the stairs and tunnels and ladders and skyscrapers and spaceships of literature spring. It will always work for you; it's not just a classroom trick to do and forget. Never is it time to cast the sentence aside; you can never get beyond it. It enables writers of term papers, love letters, memos, and corporate reports, just as it does Shakespeare.

Use: Pleasure

Grammar, any system of grammar, is fascinating. It pleases those who enjoy analysis, by its neatness, as it reduces the vast range and minute particulars of language to a coherent set. It pleases those who take joy in language, as it talks intimately and at length about what delights them. Some grammars speculate on the human mind, and so please those who like philosophy and psychology.

Grammar also pleases those who use it to learn a second or a seventh language. It works like magic as it gradually invests language new to us with the grammar-power we enjoy in our mother tongue. (Indeed, grammar—"gramarye"—used to mean magic. Grammar is kin to glamor, too. Language is full of mystery, potency, energy. Look up "grammar" in a big dictionary sometime.)

Use: Translation

Grammar as a school subject was not originally the grammar of students' mother tongue; that's a fairly recent development. Grammar was the bridge out of mother tongues into Latin and Greek, in centuries when English—or Spanish or French—had no academic standing.

Today, modern languages are important. So deeply multinational are culture and business, so close have we all become, that we measure distance in travel-time (Houston's five hours from Bogota; Vancouver's a day's drive from LA). The value of knowing many languages is plainer than ever. Consider that. And consider that you can master the abstract system of normative traditional grammar by using it concretely and actively. Let it do what it's designed for. Use it to learn another language.

Use: Conscious Control

Short of multilinguality, grammar may be of some use to you as a writer once you've written enough to trust your own grammar-power. You may add to your understanding of graphics or of syntactic possibility by reading what grammars have to say and turning a grammatically informed eye on your own writing.

And grammar is always useful to you as a copy-editor. A good book of normative grammar is a welcome reference tool. The prime time to use it is when you copy-edit your papers, after they've been rewritten and before you make a clean copy of your final version. Copy-editing is not crucial to good writing. (When F. Scott Fitzgerald gave his publishers the manuscript of *The Great Gatsby*, it contained 5,000 errors in spelling.)

Yet copy-editing is part of the writer's, or publisher's, task. A copy-editor corrected Fitzgerald's manuscript before it went to the printer. In a group where you are both writer and publisher, copy-editing final drafts is up to you. It certainly polishes the surface to a shine fit for making writing public, since it persuades readers that the writer's task has been completed. So you'll want to copy-edit your work correctly.

You'll also proofread your recopied final drafts. (Copy-editors make sure spelling, graphics, usage, and grammar are correct and consistent.) Proofreaders compare the copy-edited pages with the typed, printed, or handwritten final version, to make sure no typos or other accidental errors have crept in.

Keep a dictionary and handbooks of grammar and usage to serve your copy-editing sessions. A dictionary resolves the graphics of spelling, and—like the "lexicon" part of grammar—defines words and classifies them as parts of speech. The book of usage reassures you when you're uncertain about a phrase or expression. It's an expanded and special view of parts of the dictionary and includes some points of syntax. The grammar text reminds you what's normal in syntax and inflection. It usually describes graphic marks which conventionally punctuate grammatical structures. Graphics, though not strictly a part of grammar, are also shown in composition handbooks along with other nongrammatical matters which their authors relate to compositon.

You will want, eventually—why not now?—to choose a grammar, a dictionary, and a book of usage for your permanent personal library.

Consider the best first. Try the tools professionals use. They're clear because they have to be, and they stick to essentials.

For grammar, graphics, and usage, look at the *University of Chicago Manual of Style* (University of Chicago Press), *Words into Type* (Prentice-Hall), and *Modern English Usage* (Oxford University Press), which is a witty dictionary of tiny essays on points every writer puzzles over.

For a dictionary, you'll need a standard college edition. If you're a shaky speller, get a portable paperback too—and port it. Then save up, haunt secondhand bookstores, and when you can, invest in an unabridged dictionary—Webster's for current usage, the great 2-volume reprint of the 13-volume *Oxford English Dictionary* for its delectable histories of words.

Using a Textbook

Thousands of composition handbooks are afloat on the world's book markets. Your group may have been assigned such a text. Here's one way to get good use of it. It's also a way to examine texts when you are considering buying a reliable reference book. Try it with this book, too, though it's aimed not at reference but at active writing done by you.

Have your group consider the book together. Look at the index. (If it has no index, it may not be worth consideration as a reference.) Choose an aspect of grammar listed there.

Say you've chosen adverbs. Find the place in the text which discusses adverbs, and have someone read a page or so of it aloud, as if it were an essay of your own. Listen as you usually do when someone reads a paper. If it includes questions, examples, or exercises, read them too. Don't answer questions or exercises. Just notice what you can about them, along with the rest of the text.

Write observations on what you've heard, for 5 minutes. Have someone reread the section; write another 5 minutes of observations. Remember you're asking yourself to say not what you've learned about adverbs but what you've noticed about this particular piece of prose. You as reader are in charge here.

Read the observations aloud. Listen well for how others use this glimpse of a composition text as a real book really written for real readers.

Writing groups are busy; there's much to do, intense interest in the doing, and no time to spare. But we take time for this fresh look at a handbook, so you can discover how to read it and bring it into your service. Sadly, few of us expect a handbook to be readable, or demand that it be well enough sorted out to deserve use as a reference. See it not as rules you fear to break, but a spare, clear structure of definitions, there to steady you once you are at ease with it.

19

Writer's Proof:
Essay on an Assigned Topic

So far, you've trusted that the work of this book would get you somewhere.

You've gone over and over parts of writing which improve with practice:

- how to write fluently in search of what you know (prolific writing; making observations);
- how to write concretely (listening attentively, writing observations, dialogue in fables, family parables);
- how to write abstractly to identify our understanding of something concrete (aphorisms for fables; paragraphs of definition derived from adjectives; intuiting the structure as a whole);
- how to compose a simple expository essay, with a governing pronoun, governing tense, governing idea, and with 3 parts— beginning, middle, end (abstract idea in paragraph one, concrete example in middle, concretely enriched idea in conclusion);
- how to rewrite each part and any sentence.

Now it's time to put the work to the proof. You need to know how useful these skills have become, and to practice making them work together flexibly. Here's the chance to test them; it's also the way to practice unifying them, calling them into play together to generate expository essays on demand.

Write a simple expository essay on one of these subjects:

- nonsense
- choosing
- coincidence
- success

- quality
- generosity
- inexperience
- welcome

- vanity
- silence
- fair treatment
- foolishness

Time yourself, so that you use every one of 50 minutes to complete the essay.

In class, read your essay; listen and write and read observations on those of your colleagues. This is free practice in more than one skill at a time. Each time you pay heed to an essay, you are—without trying—reinforcing your intuitive sense of the whole structure you're working to embody. In turn, when you come to write, that intuitive sense readies your hand and mind so that what you develop word by word emerges as a poised and well-articulated unity. Reading these test essays and working on them together, you'll look again at the structuring force of appropriate language in your beginning, middle, and end passages.

You may have noticed that we haven't previously assigned or suggested subjects for your essays. That's because such subjects are best fit for testing and practicing skills already acquired, and least fit for acquiring them. So far, we've been concentrating on acquiring them.

The work this book proposes enables you to write essays both at will and on demand. The elemental skills we've set forth so far serve you when you have something in mind you'd like to write about—at will. They also serve you to set forth your ideas and concrete information when you're asked to demonstrate what you know and can do, whether on writing tests, or in this or other courses or situations—on demand.

Your next dozen essays give you essential practice in writing on demand. They put to use, all at once, the separate skills you've worked on so far.

Go back to the list, and write another essay in 50 minutes, based on one of those abstract words. Here are the steps:

Unless you know instantly what you're going to tell, choose your word, and turn it over in your mind by writing nonstop for a few minutes; you are digging for an event you can recall concretely and fully enough to bring out in the middle paragraphs, as an example of the word which is your subject.

Decide quickly on a governing pronoun.

Write sentences which define the way you want to use the word.

Then write your middle paragraphs of example.

Read over what you've written, and conclude it.

Here's a rule of conduct for you: Never stop working on your essay before the fiftieth minute has elapsed. You're practicing not a 40- or a 60-minute essay, but a 50-minute one. Speed, here, means not finishing ahead of others but filling all the time you have. Keep thinking of good things to do, and do them, on behalf of your brainchild. Readers can get out of it only as much as you put in.

We've chosen 50 minutes because it's apparently the time limit most often set for writing essay tests. You can adjust from it without strain, when necessary, because repeating the 50-minute interval many times gives you a feeling for timing—for how long it takes you to write how much. A practical sense of timing is in itself a useful skill.

Write at least one more essay on a word in the list. This process of self-testing and exercising for flexibility is yours to carry out through at least a dozen more essays. Remember that reading aloud, listening, and making observations are more vital than ever. You want to internalize the essay form deeply. By far the most efficient way to do that is the way you've worked so far: combine writing with taking in the similarly structured, different work of your colleagues.

Here's a list of fairly concrete words for you to select from:

- snapshots
- a holiday feast
- dancing
- practical jokes
- Motor Vehicle Bureau
- electronics
- grandfather
- nature lovers
- the comforts of home
- osmosis
- introductions
- Romeo and Juliet
- the kitchen table
- remembering nursery rhymes
- the school yard

Remember, one well-developed story that you enjoy thinking about is a stronger, more telling example than any list of undeveloped examples.

Write essays in 50 minutes for at least 4 of these. Once you've recalled an eventful story more or less about one of them, write it out, leaving plenty of blank space on the first page, where you'll put your first paragraph. Read over your story. Perhaps you'll use the move from adjective to noun to the definition of idea which your first sentence needs; it's quick and can't go astray. Write, in the space you left at the start, your first paragraph, defining an abstract view of the story. Read what you wrote, and compose a conclusion.

It's our experience that writing the first couple of essays to prove what you've mastered is fun, while the next couple may seem a bit tiresome or forced. That's a sign your skills are coming together and growing. By the sixth essay in this shape, most people can sense an increase in their control. To a skilled worker, work's a breeze. The skilled driver has none of the dread or anxiety of the beginner behind the wheel for the first time.

20

Writer's Proof: Essay on an Assigned Quotation

Since the skills you've practiced so far are elemental, they underlie writing of all kinds. You can adjust not only the timing of these 50-minute essays but any part you want, when you're asked to meet difficult demands.

For example, you can accommodate what you've learned to the kind of writing test which asks you to agree or disagree with the idea a quotation suggests. Such tests often look something like this:

Write an essay in which you agree or disagree with one of the following statements:

A. "The great thing in all education is to make our nervous systems our ally instead of our enemy.... We must make automatic and habitual, as early as possible, as many useful actions as we can." William James, *Principles of Psychology*

B. "On the whole, I think it cannot be maintained that dressing has in this or any country risen to the dignity of an art.... Every generation laughs at old fashions, but follows religiously the new." Henry Thoreau, *Walden*

Most of you, after practicing the work so far, can write a good response right off. There are dozens of good ways of getting started. For those who want a few concrete suggestions to dispel the tensions of test-taking, here's one sensible way:

Choose whichever quotation you feel you grasp most readily through your own experience or knowledge.

Copy the quotation quickly and accurately at the top of your page, quotation marks, author, and title of work, too, if you can do so in 2 or 3 minutes. This is an efficient, rapid way to get the thought into your head where you need it.

Use your skill in rewriting to produce in your own words another good sentence or two which says what you see it means. Include "I agree" or "I disagree" in this rewriting. Define a key word in the quotation. (For instance, "Since habits can train the nervous system to contribute to our education, I agree that we should form good habits early. Habits are actions that we do not have to stop to think about. They save us trouble.") You'll notice that the writer has used "habit," abstracted from the quotation, as the subject of her first paragraph.

Next comes the concrete development of the idea, which will be the explanatory example in the middle of the essay.

It will provide you with something more to say about your idea as a conclusion. (You'll find the whole essay about habits in Part IV, Sample Essays, pages 127–28).

Here's another example: This time, the writer wanted to use the quotation as a frame for an idea of his own which was neither pure agreement nor pure disagreement with the assigned statement. He used B, above, this way:

> "Since fashion in clothes changes quickly, I agree that it does not have the dignity of an art. But choosing how to dress is a way of showing our style, suitable for the occasion."

He was able to speak to the assigned subject by agreeing with part of it and turning the rest of it just enough in the direction of his own enthusiasm. The middle of his essay offered a paragraph on clean jeans for classroom wear and a long, intense account of juggling shopping time and budget to achieve a distinctive appearance when in public with friends.

Think of the quotation not as a jail but as a playing field. It has limits, but all kinds of moves and plays can take place within them.

Here's a point to watch for in this kind of essay: Quotations are usually chosen for their style as well as their subject; don't let yourself be hypnotized by that style. Avoid wandering into a circular maze of repeated generalizations on the theme. Make the beginning of your essay draw on your own thought. Keep the essay yours by developing the middle with the vivid, concrete expression of something you know.

Here are more quotations. Write essays based on 3 or 4 of them. Consider trying one which doesn't interest you much to start off with; this is practice-time, and you may work out your own ways to get around your own indifference. A skilled writer finds ways to enjoy writing under almost any circumstance.

> "A photograph describes everything but explains nothing."
> Honoré Daumier, *Letters*

"A man is in general better pleased when he has a good dinner upon his table than when his wife talks Greek." Samuel Johnson

"We use our parents like recurring dreams, to be entered into when needed; they are always there, to love or to hate; but it occurs to me that I was not always there for my father." Doris Lessing, *A Small Personal Voice*

"Books designed for children at the pre-school, elementary, and secondary levels should show married women who work outside the home and should treat them favorably." *Guidelines for Treatment of the Sexes in McGraw-Hill Book Company Publications*

"Political language—and with variations this is true of all political parties, from Conservatives to Anarchists—is designed to make lies sound truthful and murder respectable, and to give an appearance of solidity to pure wind." George Orwell, "Shooting an Elephant"

"Revenge is a kind of wild justice, which the more man's nature runs to, the more ought he to weed it out.... Certainly, in taking revenge, a man is but even with his enemy; but in passing it over, he is superior." Francis Bacon, *Essays*

21

Writer's Proof: Essays for Any Course or Occasion

Expository essays both help you to know what you know and to show your knowledge equitably.

You now know from experience how to write an expository essay. And you know that you know. You know how each of three parts speaks for itself and through the other parts. Your writing for purposes outside the work of this group will profit from your new awareness and control.

Deepen the authority of your skill. Use it to write thinking, expressive essays for any purpose, on any information. (Reread Chapter 2.) Take another look at the whole expository structure by turning its parts into the questions latent behind them.

The beginning answers the question: What can I assert? The middle answers the question: Of all the data I have, what supports my assertion?

The end answers the question: What does this middle choice and arrangement of data show about my assertion?

To be ready to use the questions, you know how to begin—in the middle. That is, you write nonstop to think over all the data you've learned on the subject. If you haven't enough to make sense, you find more data and learn it. (By learning, we mean putting in mind and memory. Data—off the page, from notes or experiments, etc.—must be in your head ready to recall.) Then you rummage through your data, writing nonstop, till an idea emerges.

You use the idea to answer Question 1: What can I assert? You write and rewrite the idea to make sure you've framed what your data can demonstrate and has inspired. You assert the idea. This responsible, original definition in Paragraph 1 sets up the terms for the rest of your essay.

Use the definition of Paragraph 1 to answer Question 2: Of all the data, what supports my assertion? Paragraph 1 is the filter that sifts the material you have in mind. It helps you decide on the best order for your report of the relevant facts. You write and rewrite them as ordered support for Paragraph 1.

To answer Question 3: What does the middle data show about what I assert? You read the beginning and middle, and draw a conclusion from them. Remember your work on endings, in Chapter 14. The ease with which you conclude from them tests the success of your beginning and middle parts. The elegance with which you express your conclusion conveys your success to the reader.

PART TWO

Two-Part Essay Shapes

A
FIRST SERIES

Interplay or Dialogue–Essays with a Double Voice or Point of View

22

Seed Sentences and the Two-Part Essay

Everything you really know and have lived—no matter what other people know about it or how they value it—has potency: the power to make the possible actual. Writing is one human way to exercise that power of life.

In this book you began your writing with shapes you could sense as a whole, something which begins, turns, and concludes. The shape (Fable or Parable) gave you an idea for writing. That is, it showed you the possibility of connecting life and thinking.

You became skilled: first at writing whatever you chose, and then at writing on topics, tests of what you know and how you say it.

Now we turn away from testing to show you other ways of writing essays. Again, you begin with your sense of a whole shape. Once again, your sense of the shape gives you an idea. This time the idea of the shape is contained in a single sentence, like a seed. Not a topic sentence, of course, because topics are general. They are commonplaces. A seed sentence is a literary idea; it's concrete-abstract. It contains the *structure* of the essay; that's the abstract part. The special language of your seed sentence is the concrete part. Your own essay is your original definition of the idea.

The seed sentences show that the essays all have two-part shapes. You can play one part off against the other, sometimes by balanced coordination, sometimes by subordinating one part to the other. (See Chapter 8.) The second part seems to start things over again from another point of view. One part begins the idea; the other part concludes it; and the way they interplay gives the idea its special turn.

The essay parts are unified by their shape, for the power of shape or form is unity, the way it helps you make your writing interesting all the way through. The parts get their interest not from their own sparkle but by the way they fit together into the whole.

But the best thing about your seed sentences is that they let you begin *directly*, without trying to find a subject and "cook" it ahead of time. You begin each essay by writing four or five sentences, each a version of the essay shape. You can't do them wrong (this is not a test). Then you simply choose your most promising sentence and open it up into an essay.

23

Once/Now: The Essay of Reflection

Write 4 or 5 seed sentences of your own like these:

- Once I was shy; now I'm mellow.
- Once I was a grass-green country boy; now I survive in the Bronx.
- Once I was a student; now I'm a salesperson.
- Once I was a junk-food fan, but now I'm a health-food nut.

Read all the sentences of your group aloud and enjoy listening to them, but don't interrupt them for comments. Whenever the sentences you hear give you more ideas, write more sentences.

Notice one thing about all the sample sentences: the verbs on both sides are positive: *was* shy/*am* mellow. A sentence with a negative would look like this: *was* shy/*no* longer shy (or *not* shy). In the negative version, there's only one seed word: *shy*, and it appears on both sides of the sentence. In the original version, there are two seed words: *shy* and *mellow*. Read your sentences over to make sure that both sides are positive, each side having its own seed word.

Pick your best seed sentence and begin writing an essay with this as your first sentence. Write for 5 minutes nonstop about the *Once* part of the sentence.

Write for 5 more minutes on the *Now* part of the sentence.

Read these essays around the group. After each writer reads, write observations for 1 minute about how the essay is written or designed. Begin with the obvious or what you remember most strongly.

When all the essays have been read, call for listeners to read observations about each essay. You might want to write down some of the observations you hear about your own essay. Don't interrupt the observations for comments; you want to make sure each essayist hears observations. You also want to be sure to hear all the observations possible from the group; what someone notices about another essay may give you a good idea about your own. None of these observations, of course, are opinions, evaluations, or suggestions. They represent what your listeners noticed. Think about them and draw your own conclusions.

Take your essay home and expand each of its two parts along the lines you began in class. Rewrite and reorganize what you've already written if that seems good to you. When you've finished, reread the essay and give it a good title.

For your next assignment, look over your stock of seed sentences and choose another good one as the first sentence of a two-part Once/Now essay.

Seed Sentence into First Paragraph

You've written a brief essay which is the liveliest and most memorable form of an experience you could call up in a short period of writing. Your next move is to take the seed sentence and expand it into a new first paragraph.

As always, read your essay again, to think about how it worked out. Then rewrite the seed sentence in several versions to make it more fitting for what you actually said. When you have the best sentence, keep writing for 4 or 5 more sentences to get a good first paragraph that displays the idea in its whole shape, in its main parts, and in the way it's tending. (Give no details yet.) The paragraph will show that "noticeable ordering and division of its parts" we spoke of earlier (in Chapter 2) as the marks of an expository essay.

Here's an example. The original seed sentence was, "Once I was just a working girl; now I'm back to being a student." This is the new first paragraph:

> Once I was a working girl with much free time on my hands; now I'm also a student with self-discipline and a strict work schedule. I used to come home in the evening, and my time was my own. I enjoyed socializing and keeping myself fit with sports and my weekly dance class. I did as I pleased and never had to be anywhere at any specific time. Now I have to say, "No, I can't make it tonight; I have an assignment to do." It's not quite as simple as it sounded when I said, "I'll have to sacrifice, but I'll do it, and it won't be so hard. I just won't go out as much as I do now."

Put your new first paragraph at the head of your original brief essay. Read over these two parts. Then write an ending to say something conclusive about the idea of your first paragraph, after the evidence of the middle of the essay. You need 4 or 5 sentences for a good ending.

Turn to Chapter 12 of this book to review the idea of a unified essay. For rewriting the essay, begin with Chapter 14. When you've done the writing described there, proceed to Chapters 16 and 17.

24

Observations on the Essay

Observing and Paying Attention

If you find yourself falling into the habit of restating the points of an essay you hear or criticizing it instead of writing your observations, you can renew your sense of how observations work by turning to the work described in Chapters 7 and 13. If there's no aphorism from a fable handy, recall a fine sentence from a recent essay. Copy it as the author rereads it. Then make a list of what you notice about how the sentence is written. For example, in this sentence, "She burnt her coal without warming herself," I notice that the sentence turns on the negative word *without*. Take 2 minutes and write nonstop. Begin with the obvious. Read all these observations around the room and enjoy listening to them, without interrupting them for comment.

As you write about a single sentence, it's easy to see that you don't have to paraphrase or summarize it for other readers. The art of a well-written sentence appears because you can see the whole sentence, and all its ways of working together, at once. Your aim now is to hear the essay as well as you read the sentence. Perfect your aim by focusing on what you actually hear. You don't have to "cover" the essay or say everything important about it. It's enough to speak of what you "see" when you listen.

Listening actively is one of the skills of reading. When you read silently, the listening power goes inside, into the mind, and becomes attention.

Take 10 minutes now and write nonstop about your own experiences of reading aloud and listening. Read this. Write for 10 minutes nonstop on what you've learned from observations on your writing. Read.

Observing and Evaluating

If you don't evaluate essays, what do you get out of paying so much attention to them?

The first thing you get from listening to observations is the chance to draw your own conclusions about what you hear. Each of you has limited what you wrote to a moment or two of plain description of what you heard. You chose rapidly two or three things to say, which means you left a lot unsaid. What you did not say is just as much information to the writer as what you did say.

Of course, you hear what your colleagues have written in quite a different way than they see it. They're still seeing a good deal that they did not actually write. Observations often surprise the authors but seldom the listeners. Authors are reading a *first version* of their idea. They have more to get out of an idea that only they can see. Evaluation at this stage is crippling.

Authors need listeners to recognize and describe the effective and memorable parts of what they have written so that they can develop their individual ways of writing. That's what *original* means: not "unlike any other writing" (that's impossible) but "originating from an individual point of view."

Reading Aloud

Reading aloud is energizing. Knowing you have listeners for your writing brings it to life even in its first stages of composition. And when you read, you hear your essay in a new way, because you're soaking up some of the listening power of your listeners.

The difficult, hard-to-say, knotty passages of your writing bother you when you try to read them aloud. Phony language stands out bare naked when you say it in your own voice. Writers who never read their work aloud can struggle for a whole semester with mixed-up sentences and clotted paragraphs, and still be unable to move their writing out into the easy, colloquial flow of language that is the glory of English prose.

Problems with mixed-up sentences are usually superficial, in our experience, though they attract a lot of attention from worried teachers and writers. By *superficial* we mean problems that are merely part of the awkwardness of inexperience. Fussing with them is a waste of time and a distraction from the real job of writing steadily. After you've read three or four essays aloud, some of the flow of speaking will enter your writing and wash away the stiff and stilted parts.

"This is too optimistic," you say? "My problems won't clear up so quickly—I'm too poor a writer for that." Maybe. And maybe some writing problems are caused by poor assignments and poor class conduct. Then work designed to *cure* the problems it is *causing* becomes a vicious circle.

Reading aloud, listening, writing observations, and reading them are a set of actions, and the power is in the set. They work irresistibly together if you engage them.

What I've Noticed and Learned about Listening

1. Listening is easier and more entertaining than reading.
2. Listening is continuous. Part of its pleasure is freedom from interruption; part of its instruction is to be steady.
3. Individual differences among essays are much sharper when I listen to them than when I read them.
4. What I notice seems bright or spacious to me when I listen.
5. As I listen, awkward or general writing fades out of my attention.
6. I always hear something new or ingenious. And as I do, I recognize it as something I know from a great writer. That recognition increases my pleasure in the new author and the old.
7. Recalling a piece of writing, I find it has reordered itself in my mind, the brightest and best parts coming first.

At first, from such experiences I concluded that listening and writing are two different powers. Now I think it makes more sense to say that writing is two pieces of writing at the same time. One we get by listening, the other by reading. The printed part makes the essay look finished (or as if it ought to be finished). The listening part gives us glimpses into the idea behind the writing, the possibilities of the writing. I've learned that it's a lot easier to miss or lose the part of writing we get by listening.

The eye loves correct and polished writing. It expects a fine or easy surface, and it's quick to find faults. But the writing we hear has no surface yet. It's breathing and finding a voice, a shape, a direction.

I've learned that change and development come from this part of writing, the part writers can listen to and hear. Listening makes rewriting imaginable.

The essay we hear has potential, a power not yet spent. We can hear what hasn't yet been realized by the author, a still possible version of the essay. And when writers can imagine rewriting, they can proceed as real writers do: to find out what they still owe their idea.

25

The Seed Sentence as a Question

You've used the seed sentence as an idea to start you writing. The special structure of the sentence lets you see a shape you could give your experience. Then the shape helps you think more about the experience.

If you change the seed sentence slightly you can see its analytical use. Change its language from concrete to abstract and general, and change its form from assertion to question. For example, change "Once I was a working girl who spent her time as she pleased; now I'm also a student with a strict schedule," to "How does one thing look under contrasting conditions?" "Time" and "schedule" in the seed sentence are generalized to "one thing" in the question; and "working girl"/"as she pleased" and "student"/"strict" become "contrasting conditions." The *Once/Now* essay, if you look at it abstractly to see its structure, is a way of thinking about how one thing looks under contrasting conditions.

When you get to know a literary shape by writing it yourself, you can use its power to let you see and think about anything you've learned. Though the *language* of a test question is general, its *shape* is abstracted from a special image, so the question demands a specific answer. The shape of the question tells you what must be the shape of your answer.

Most tests feature general and abstract language. Unfortunately, tight knots of abstract and general language paralyze most people (even those who make up the test). And, again unfortunately, test questions seem to send a message: "You must write your answer like this question."

The first thing to know about writing essays, either as examinations or as assigned topics, then, is that you do not have to write your answer in the *language* of the question. In its *shape*, yes, but not in its very generalized language. You don't want to paralyze your reader. The next thing to know is that you've written this shape successfully before, in one of its concrete forms. The test question is nothing more than the abstract form of one of your own essays.

Think of these essays, yours and your colleagues', and the artful ways they work. You don't invent your material for a test (as you did for your *Once/Now* essay), but you always invent ways of making your writing a pleasure to read.

To help you see relations between your own essays and the analyses you may be asked to write, we give you the analytical question for each essay shape. In fact, you'll find the questions useful yourself to ask about your own essays, when you want to rewrite and develop them.

The question for the Once/Now essay is:

HOW DOES ONE THING LOOK UNDER CONTRASTING CONDITIONS?

Sample test question:

Admiral Rickover contends that we should sometimes say *no* to a new technological advancement. It appears that the other authors agree with him, but there are differences in their views. Discuss what three of these four authors say about the conditions under which a society or individual should say *no* to a new technological development.

Don't ever let the length of a test question or its general language faze you. Your answer doesn't have to sound like that. This question is the one implied by the first essay shape: "How does one thing look under contrasting conditions?" The "one thing" is "saying *no* to a new technological development."

Recall how you wrote your Once/Now essays. Check your seed sentence to make sure all three parts are expressed positively, each with its own key word. Cross out negatives that simply indicate what one author does *not* say. Negatives always creep in when you're trying to think of what you want to say, but they're deadwood on a test. Toss them out.

Since the answer calls for three conditions, write a three-part essay. Finish one part before you begin the next part. Remember that as you line up your thoughts for one part, your mind is already using that as a pattern, racing ahead to find thoughts that will fit into the next part. As you write the first part, your mind is already composing the second and third parts.

That kind of composing goes on readily when you begin with the author or idea that interests you the most (not with the one you happened to read first or the one mentioned first in a question). Always begin with the attractive center of your thought.

You gain mastery of the author's world by speaking the language of that world. For example, in Plato's dialogue called *Crito*, Socrates habitually uses the word *agree*: "And, Crito, you must be careful in agreeing to this, not to say that you agree unless you really do." Using Socrates' special words for what he means helps make your answer specific and alive with the life in language of a special thought.

26

"They Say":
The Essay of Testing

Imagine yourself at a party, or at a new school or new job with people who don't know you. In the course of a conversation, you get enthusiastic about the sports you do, and your listener says, "Oh, you must be a jock." Here are more sentences like that:

- "You're in therapy? You don't *look* sick."
- "It must have been pretty boring growing up in a small town."
- "You live in New York? How many times you been mugged?"
- "We all know what Italians are like."

Write 3 or 4 sentences like these. When you've finished, read them aloud to your colleagues and listen to theirs. If you haven't thought of several good sentences, what you hear will remind you of some. Jot them down.

Reread your sentences and pick the one you can expand in order to say more of what "they" say. Write nonstop for 5 minutes what "they" say. Don't jump in with your own side of the question yet.

At home, complete your essay in two parts: "They *say* that, but my *experience* is this." Don't argue. Reason isn't known by the way it wins arguments, but by the way it tests. The mark of reason is that it brings opinion to the test. Let ignorance have its say—and let it expose itself.

Then it's your turn. Show the actual, living experience of the situation—your insider's knowledge of the circumstances. Be sure your part of the essay is concrete.

At your next meeting, read your essays aloud to each other. After each essay write 1 minute nonstop your observations of how that essay is written. Hold on to these observations, but don't interrupt the reading of the essays by comment or discussion. After the essays, read your observations to the authors.

*   *   *

The elemental question for the "They Say" essay is:

WHAT ASSUMPTION IS THE OPPOSITION DEPENDING ON?

Sample test question:

George Innes suggests that Impressionism is painting by "scientific formula," and that it fails as art because it denies the importance of feeling. Having read the remarks in these readings by Impressionists themselves and by other critics, would you consider Innes's assertion fully correct, partially correct, or incorrect?

Most test questions try to help the student, and it's a good idea to look for the helpful parts. This question is useful in identifying the assumption of Innes: that Impressionism is painting by "scientific formula." It even elaborates that assumption, just as we suggested you do when you began your "They Say" essay: "...it fails as art because it denies the importance of feeling."

To organize your answer as a two-part essay, you'd develop Innes's assumption as fully as you could first. The easiest way of doing that is to use his language. We don't mean quote passages, but use his special words and little phrases when you lay out what he's talking about. You did this naturally when you wrote your essays because you sensed that the wrong parts of what people say are easier to locate in their own language. And you were right. As you use your opponents' language, you get a better and better sense of where it depends on assumptions that your own knowledge tells you are shaky.

Writing a New Final Paragraph

You can use the question form of the seed sentence for each essay shape to compose a new conclusion to the core of your essay. A conclusion, you recall, tells the difference the middle makes to the idea of the beginning. It offers a fuller view of the idea. It shows how the middle has developed the sense of the beginning.

Reread your "They Say" essay with its new first paragraph. Ask yourself the question form of the seed sentence: What is the crucial assumption my opposition was depending on? Name the assumption in a word. Thinking of your experience, write a sentence to say why the assumption was crucial. Rewrite the sentence in three different versions. Then continue writing to complete your thought.

27

Same Subject?

Suppose you find yourself coming back to the same subject no matter what the assignment. Then that's your genius. Make it welcome.

> TEAM TEACHER: If Fred writes another essay about jogging, I'm going to scream!
>
> R: What's wrong with that?
>
> T.T.: What if they're all about jogging? It'll be boring. You know they're boring.
>
> R: Yes, but I'm not bored.
>
> T.T.: Not even if they're all about jogging?
>
> R: Even the greatest writers have one theme that they spend their whole lives exploring and thinking about.
>
> T.T.: They had important subjects to think about.
>
> R: They kept on writing till they made a world out of their subject.
>
> T.T.: But who would want a world of jogging?
>
> R: The beauty of any world is that it's coherent and ample.
>
> T.T.: You can't do that with jogging.
>
> R: Have you noticed that writing is like jogging? You do it and keep on doing it and go a little farther every day, farther than necessary, farther than customary. Fred is going to master writing the same way he's mastered jogging.
>
> T.T.: Well, he'll have to show me.

Did Fred write all his essays about jogging? Yes, for almost two semesters. Did he master writing? The last time we saw him, he was going strong and not out of breath yet.

28

Two Voices:
The Essay of Comic Liberty

Sometimes you agree to disagree with a friend. She likes the country; you like the city. She likes quiet, ironic people; you prefer talkative, sociable ones. She likes cats; you like dogs. Write some sentences like these:

- In my family there are the early risers and the late sleepers.
- My co-worker's desk is so crowded with equipment and plants that she has to sit side-saddle. My desk is bare except for one folder of work.
- They spend their holidays getting briny and baked on the sea sands, but we retreat to the cool quiet of mountain shade and mountain streams.
- He's an only child who got all his parents' attention, but I'm for the fights and fun of a large family.

These are seed sentences for the third essay, which says: "You can do it another way, but you can also do it in this way." Write one voice for 5 minutes. Then write the other voice for 5 minutes. Complete the essay at home as a two-part essay. As you usually do, bring your completed essays to your meeting and read them aloud to each other. Write 1 or 2 minutes of observations after each essay, but don't interrupt your listening for comment.

*   *   *

If there's a dialogue in which one side is mistaken while the other side knows better, there must be a dialogue where each side is right in its own way. Your last essay gave priority to one side, showed one side more authentic than the other. This essay discovers differences among equals: shows how each view is authentic. That's what a simple comparison is.

That doesn't mean that both sides have to be equally valuable to the author. One set of values may be hers, and she may openly prefer it. (You'll notice this in many of the essays you heard.) But she can see the difference and make the distinction. She doesn't have to set up one side by knocking down the other.

In non-writing classes, when the teacher asks for an essay comparing two things, the weakest essay always turns out to be the one that fails to see the interest of the difference. It's too busy praising one thing at the expense of another. But then it doesn't even do justice to the thing it prefers. In learning or study, it's important to be able to make a fair distinction between two things, each of which is good in its own way.

That isn't hard to learn in this assignment, as you noticed when you listened to all the essays read aloud. We call this essay, "Comic Liberty," though that doesn't mean that it must be funny. By *comic* we mean the spirit of the happy ending of comedy, which, you notice, has a good deal of forgiveness and acceptance in it. And by *liberty* we mean free of envy or self-interest, a freedom we've always noticed in the essays we get from this assignment.

As you listen to your colleagues' essays and write your observations, pay special attention to all their ways of seeing a fair difference.

For your next assignment, write another Two-Voices essay.

*   *   *

The elemental question for the Two-Voices essay is:

SOME SEE IT THIS WAY; SOME SEE IT THAT WAY. TO WHAT EXTENT IS EACH VALID?

Sample test question:

Some see the effects of television as stemming from its content. Others emphasize the nature of the medium itself. With specific reference to the readings, discuss the extent to which each of these positions is valid.

This question is simpler than the first two sample questions, but it's more demanding: "discuss the extent" sounds hard. But that's simply the effect of the general language of tests. The question is helpful because it defines the two parts of the answer: the content and the medium. Always look to the *structure* of a test question for help. Help yourself by changing the *language* of the test from general to specific or concrete. In this question "content" and "medium" are the two voices of the answer.

In a test situation recall the essays you have written and heard. You probably noticed two things: the order in which the two sides, the two voices, appear and the language of each voice.

Perhaps you began your own essay with the voice you sympathized with most. Do that when you write about study material because it gives you a strong start. Don't just discuss what you read in the order in which you happen to read it. Do begin with what you know and like best. That helps you to reorder in your own mind what you read. That reordering is one sign that you're mastering it.

Speak the language of the reading when you write about it. You did that before when you wanted to show the weakness of what "they" say. Here you want to show the strength; use the same technique. When you think about what people say using their own language, you'll discover the weakness of their notions when the language is weak, and the strength of their thought when their language has power.

29

The Turning Point
of a Writing Course

Each set of seed sentences you write springs out of one idea: an image of your experience. An idea *is* an image (*idea*, from the Greek *idon: seen*), something you see in your mind's "eye." Part memory, it's also part perception because you're seeing the experience now—with what you now know and value. So the experience has more reality now than when it happened. It has the added "reality of proportion and perspective."*

You and your readers sense this added or greater reality in your writing: in its vividness, liveliness, the way its parts fit together, the rightness of its order, its fine sentences. This greater reality in the writing is what we call *literature* and what we mean when we say you are writing literature. Your essays are as literary as novels, poems, plays. There's a whole rainbow of literature from poetry at one edge to analytic literature at the other, and no one who's reading the whole rainbow can say just where an essay on biology or anthropology becomes literature any more than where red becomes violet, and violet becomes blue. Any "single" color comes in infinite tones and hues. The form of the essay, like the color yellow, has infinite variety.

Sometimes in a school writing course the pressure builds up; authors are told, "Now you must stop writing literature and write seriously, write real analysis, real essays." No, you don't have to stop writing literature. There's no such division between literature and seriousness, between analysis and literature. Often at this point authors get their writing taken away from them, are stripped of their author's authority, as teachers and peers tell them how to revise their work.

There's a true story showing what happens when writers believe in the separation of school writing from literature. A student in a literature class for non-majors was one of my most intelligent readers of literature. Though it wasn't a writing class, there was

*"...the reality of proportion and perspective, of seeing what it's all about...." Northrop Frye, *The Educated Imagination*. Indiana University Press, 1969, p. 78.

plenty of brief writing. Because this person's writing always shone with her own intelligence, I looked forward to reading it always.

Then I asked her to put several brief pieces together into a longer essay where she could work out the connections of her idea. She must have thought this was "serious" writing, and what she gave me was a disaster, all beautifully typed on excellent bond paper. Her own voice was gone; she thought serious writing isn't personal— has to be written as if there's no one there. Her vivid language was gone, so I lost the sense of the energy and pleasure of her thinking. And all her assertions were dressed up in funny, stilted academic clichés or big generalizations. The gleams of her original ideas were all but buried in the sand of her prose. And that effect had cost her a lot of trouble and time to achieve.

If there's no crisis in a writing course, then why do writers feel one? There is a turning point in a writing course: not from writing "literature" to writing "essays," but from writing at will to writing at will *and* on demand. It's passing into mastery, and it means you can write well in brief and at length, and that you can write, in your own voice, about ideas you yourself generate as well as about assigned subjects or test questions.

Some of your assignments will be for analysis. You are well able to write analytic literature. Chapters 19, 20, and the analytic question sections following each of the six essay shapes are specially designed for practice in writing analysis.

But the power to *generate* writing lies near the concrete pole of writing. Writers look at the concrete images of what they actually know in order to see the abstract structure of their knowledge. If writers bypass their own perceptions—the look, feel, taste of experience—they let slip a bit of the truth and head for a sand pit instead of a pot of gold. The gold is the greater reality, the proportion and perspective of our lives within our power to express by writing. It's the literature of our lives.

B
SECOND SERIES

Overview—Essays with a Single Voice or Point of View

30

Hindsight:
The Essay of Interpretation

Differences are interesting. Why is there one silent person in a family of talkers, or one teacher in a family of farmers? Why does one family seek change, while another seeks satisfaction? Why does one social group work beautifully in a way that another group can't tolerate?

These questions have no simple cause and effect answers. We can't know for certain why we are the way we are, either as individuals or groups. But we can think about a source in the past of the pattern we see now. Write 4 or 5 seed sentences like these:

- I'm helpful and bossy because I'm the oldest child.
- My love of old houses goes back to a chiming clock and a sunlit kitchen.
- I'm studying math instead of building houses because my father, the carpenter, always said, "Work with your head instead of your hands."

- As the middle child, I always wanted to be different.
- I've learned to trust myself, like my mother, an optimist who was never afraid of adventure.

Listen to all the sentences written by your group. Pick your own most interesting sentence. Write for 10 minutes concretely about the source in the past of the pattern you see now. Describe the action or scene that springs to your mind as vividly as possible. Let your reader see its motive power through your eyes.

In the essays of the second series, it's no longer enough simply to match the two parts, to say, "I do this (or refuse to do it) because my father always did it." A single force or point of view in the governing part of the essay now becomes active and acts on the other part. In this essay, the action is like a motive. You can't explain it, but you can show it. *Show* the fun, the satisfaction, the pride, pleasure, or need that made you keep—or reject—some pattern from the past.

*   *   *

The question form of the Essay of Hindsight is:

WHAT IS THE SOURCE OF THIS SIGNIFICANT PATTERN?

Sample test question:

In spite of equal opportunity legislation, several of the authors in this set of readings maintain that men have continued to enjoy "favored status" in the workplace. Basing your answer on specific references to the assigned readings, identify the major historical and social circumstances which have contributed to this pattern of inequality.

The test question is: What is the source of "this pattern of inequality"? What pattern of inequality? "This" one, the one everyone seems to be talking about. The most common way of going wrong on a question like this is to think you don't have to describe the "pattern of inequality" because everyone knows what it means and there's some general agreement about what the phrase refers to. There isn't. If there were, the question wouldn't have to be asked. Make sure your answer describes exactly what significant pattern you intend to discuss.

The other part of your answer describes the source and shows it as a moving power.

31

Reading Aloud and Listening

It's important that all the authors read all their writing aloud to fellow writers who listen with interest and attention. Don't omit this because you're writing longer or more complex essays.

OBJECTOR: But I'm used to *reading* a copy of the essay.

R: What do you remember after you've read them?

O: I don't have to remember—the essay's right there.

R: Where do you start with your observations?

O: With the beginning.

R: Do you find yourself making judgments before you've read the whole thing?

O: I notice where ideas aren't clear or where the beginning needs to be more catchy.

R: You read as a critic, then?

O: Sure. But I also suggest how something could be done better.

R: The critic has more authority than the author?

O: Don't authors need help?

R: They need attention and response, certainly.

O: They need to know their faults.

R: Does that embarrass authors? Or take over their writing?

O: Well, they have to be able to take criticism. But we could leave the author's name off the essay.

R: So then the author disappears altogether?

O: But we're all learning from each other's mistakes.

R: I admire you. Most people get bored with discussion of mistakes they themselves don't make.

O: It *is* a little boring. But at least the author learns from his mistakes.

R: He does? Did you ever make the same mistake over and over?

O: Yes, I guess so. But in that case, how *do* I learn?

R: From developing your strengths.

O: How do I know what they are?

R: They're the parts of your writing that attract your listeners right away and give them most pleasure. You get observations about them because they're memorable.

O: Suppose my listeners don't remember anything?

R: That's suggestive.

O: You mean I can figure it out for myself?

R: I think you can.

O: But suppose I'm not good at writing?

R: You started out by implying you were good at criticism. You don't mean to tell me that criticism is easier than writing?

O: But you're implying it's easier to learn from the success of others than from your own mistakes.

R: I do think that success is more fun than failure.

O: Even someone else's success?

R: It's your pleasure when you listen. You learn writing from pleasure in writing. Good writing makes good observations too.

O: So we're all successful?

R: The shapes you're working on—fable, parable, essay—they're all beautiful forms. They contain as many possibilities of success as you can imagine.

O: I'm not resisting success.

R: I didn't *think* you were.

O: Reading aloud is important?

R: Sound is alive, you know, in a way that print isn't. And language is alive: every sentence you hear has just been invented by its speaker.

O: Well, I can listen better than anyone in my anthropology class now. I don't know whether I can write better, though.

R: Luckily, you don't have to. Nothing could be better than your own kind of good writing.

32

Foresight: The Essay of Planning

Foresight is how you imagine what you carry out. It's about ways of getting to your goal: how you planned what you wanted. Write 4 or 5 seed sentences like these:

- When I chose my high school, I had to decide between staying with my friends and getting the courses I wanted.
- In order to go back to college, I had to re-educate my family.
- I realized that I'd have to ask my father to help me get a job, even though I never got along with him.
- It all started when my brother said, "You better figure out the *whole* cost of a new car before you buy one."

Listen to all the sentences of your group. Choose your best sentence and write for 5 minutes nonstop on your goal, what you wanted. The image of the goal is a powerful part of this essay, so write about it concretely. Then write for 5 minutes concretely on your plans. Complete this essay at home as a two-part essay.

As you write to foresee the goal, the means to the goal come into view—or the obstacles to the goal begin to appear. You notice in the essays of your group when you listen to them, how the goal or end governs the means to the end. When the goal is clear, the essay writer figures out the means to the end: "In order to get back to college, I had to re-educate my family." When there are incompatible goals, the writer chooses between them: "I had to decide between staying with my friends and getting the courses I wanted." Where there's a conflict between the means and the end, as in the last 2 sample sentences, the writer has to work harder on his plans or accept a less "expensive" goal.

Read all the essays of your group aloud, and write observations for 1 minute after each one. We often notice a greater variety of development in the composition of this essay shape than in any so far.

*   *   *

The question form of the Essay of Foresight is:

WHAT IS THE GOAL AND HOW DO YOU PLAN TO REACH IT?

The question form of the Essay of Foresight is:

WHAT IS THE GOAL AND HOW DO YOU PLAN TO REACH IT?

Sample test question:

Suppose that you were an administrator in a major hospital which has decided to computerize fully its services, including applications ranging from billing to diagnosis. With specific references to the assigned readings, indicate the dangers you would foresee as a result of this decision, and indicate the steps you would recommend to assure that the system was both as efficient and as humane as possible.

This test question is strong on letting writers imagine a situation and speak about it in their own voices. The question also defines the goal for the writer: making a certain system both efficient and humane.

As you did with your own Foresight essay, you'd begin by describing the goal, using data found in your readings. It's the reality of a purpose that lends urgency to planning.

"Wisdom Literature" in ancient times expresses the sense that in the big worlds of social reality and natural seasons, time and events do not wait for individuals to be ripe. They must foresee their ripening by planning. And they have opportunities: "To everything there is a season, and a time for every purpose under heaven." To keep on envisioning the purpose makes it easier to plan ways to realize it.

33

Insight: The Essay of Judgment

In the Essay of Foresight, your choice was made, your goal was ahead of you. Your job was to decide the means to the end, and you decided on the basis of interest or self-interest. Now we move to something more fundamental: how you choose the goal itself.

We make long-term or fundamental choices on the basis of tradition, principle, or policy. Write 3 or 4 seed sentences like these:

- I was scared, but I remember my grandmother saying, "Tell the truth and you won't get hurt."
- Was it too late to go back to school when I'd be 35 before I got a degree? I decided: I'm going to be 35 anyway; I might as well be 35 and have a degree.
- I knew I could never start because in the game of love and commitment there wasn't supposed to be an end, only an ever-after.

Have all the sentences read aloud and listen to them attentively without interruption. If listening gives you more ideas for sentences of your own, write them.

Write for 5 minutes concretely on the problem or situation part of the essay. Then write for 5 minutes concretely on the tradition or principle you turned to. At home, expand and complete the essay.

For your next assignment, choose another seed sentence and write another Essay of Insight.

*   *   *

The question form of the Essay of Insight is:

WHAT IS THE SITUATION AND WHAT PRINCIPLE OR POLICY GOVERNS IT?

Sample test question:

Write an essay which suggests a policy for dealing with ancient art, both works which have already been discovered and works yet to be found. Base your essay on specific references to the assigned reading.

This is probably the most general or comprehensive of the sample test questions: "a policy *dealing with....*" But it has two definite requests: for a *policy* and for an understanding of the *problem* of discovering ancient art. Your sense of the strategy of the Essay of Insight would enable you to write a good answer.

You'd begin by envisioning the situation, just as you did in your own essay, because a decision depends on how you see the problem. Go to the part of the readings that convinced you of the importance of the problem. The more concretely or factually you see the situation, the more likely you are to see the policy that fits.

A broad question always tempts inexperienced writers to write generally or to summarize what they've read. Nothing could be worse, for it's the very bigness or vagueness of a situation that makes it seem insoluble.

On a test of reading, you bring into play all the skills you've developed in listening, paying attention, and making observations. Instead of summarizing, find the center, the powerful and memorable idea at the heart of the readings. Define it—just as you defined your own central idea when you composed new first paragraphs for your rewritten essays.

Speak the language of the reading as you define an author's key idea. You've noticed by now that test questions always want you to make "specific reference to the assigned readings." The most direct way of doing this, of showing your authoritative familiarity with the texts and of defining the idea accurately, is to speak the language of the texts.

OVERVIEW OF THE SIX ESSAY SHAPES

Essay Shape	Literary Type	Analytical Type
Essay 1: *Once/Now* "Once I was shy; now I'm mellow."	*Autobiography* "If I should attempt to tell how I have desired to spend my life in years past...."	*Contrast* How does one thing look under contrasting conditions?
Essay 2: *They Say* "You're in therapy? You don't *look* sick."	*Satire* "Sometimes a war is entered upon because the enemy is too strong, and sometimes because he is too weak."	*Testing* What assumption is the opposition depending on?
Essay 3: *Two Voices* "In my family there are the early risers and the late sleepers."	*Comic Liberty* "You can do it another way, but you can also do it this way."	*Comparison* Some see it this way, some that way. To what extent is each valid?
Essay 4: *Hindsight* "As the middle child, I always wanted to be different."	*History/Elegy* "I took the one less traveled by, And that has made all the difference."	*Tracing the Source* What is the source of this significant pattern?
Essay 5: *Foresight* "In order to go back to school, I had to reeducate my family."	*Wisdom Literature* "To everything there is a season, and a time for every purpose under heaven."	*Planning* What is the goal, and how do you plan to reach it?
Essay 6: *Insight* "I was scared, but my grandmother said, 'Tell the truth and you won't get hurt.' "	*Law (Irony/Tragedy)* "They have sown the wind, and they shall reap the whirlwind."	*Finding the Principle* What is the situation, and what principle or policy governs it?

34

Trial Sentences

The sentence concentrates power. In this book we often ask you to write a set of single sentences. The set is an idea, and each sentence in the set is a version of that idea, an attempt to see the idea, put it in the best perspective, or think more clearly about it. By now you've written and rewritten sets of: aphorisms (Chapter 6), defining sentences (Chapter 11), and seed sentences (Chapters 22, 25, 27, 29, 31, 32).

Writing sets of sentences in this way is complementary to Prolific Writing, where sentences flow one into another and the idea seems to expand and lead to other ideas. In a set of trial sentences, each sentence returns to the key idea to try it again, define it again, find the real point of it. You try to center the point and keep it apart from a flow of associations which might diffuse it before you get a good look at it.

You always need both kinds of writing: Prolific Writing for the fluency that embodies an idea in its range and in its special music or rhythm; and Rewriting (of which trial sentences are a special form). Analysis, especially, is accomplished in two stages. The first stage is a synthesis of your observations and interpretations into an idea, working with what you sense is the most important thing. In the second stage you analyze your idea by defining it, sorting it out, finding the best parts in the best order.

In this chapter we show you more techniques for trial sentences, first for simple definition and then for double definition or comparison. All these techniques are kinds of *re*writing. They work efficiently when you have begun with some pages of writing, when the idea is already sketched out in language. The beauty of rewriting is that it works from *within* the writer's idea.

Simple Definition

A. To Identify the Parts of an Essay

You have a draft or a first version or brief essay. Somewhere in it is the key to your idea, the most interesting parts of it.

Read over your writing—several times if necessary to get it well in mind. *Now put it aside.*

Write, in one sentence, the most interesting idea of the essay. (This is a fresh sentence written without consulting the wording of the original.) Quickly write 3 more versions of this sentence. Read them.

Now in another sentence write the second most interesting thing in the essay. Write 2 or 3 more versions of the sentence. Read them.

Finally, in one sentence say what these two ideas have in common. You're trying to find the simplest relationship between them. Try 4 or 5 versions of this sentence. Begin each sentence simply by saying, "In both these ideas...." It isn't important to say what you mean perfectly or say something important in every sentence, but to keep writing nonstop for 5 minutes at least.

Read this all over and you'll find you're ready for a good rewriting of your essay.

B. To Name the Subject of an Essay

Read over your essay attentively. Ask yourself, "What was my subject and what is my special idea about it?" Choose a word or a phrase that best names your subject and make this word the subject of a set of 4 or 5 sentences. Examples:

- Winter isolated me, as if I were a hermit in the midst of the city.
- Winter keeps me busy working at a slow pace and living at a slow pace also.
- Winter is the sad experience of a visitor all dressed up for the cold and yet with a feeling of cold inside.
- Winter makes me hibernate in my room and adopt a very silent attitude.
- Winter looks so grey and sad that visitors and friends seem not to be around.
- Winter stayed with me all year round, made me ignore the birds flying back.

Winter is a fairly concrete word. Here's a set of sentences beginning with a more abstract word: *homesickness*:

- Homesickness tints the landscape speeding past the windows wan grey and green, drains the wheatfields of their gold, and sets each cow to stand alone.
- Homesickness makes each other town anonymous, its citizens shallow and claimless.
- Homesickness jabs me with each turn to remind me I should have been nicer when I was home.

- Homesickness romanticizes the past and diminishes the glitter of the future.
- Homesickness silences my carefully cultivated conversation.
- Homesickness excuses me from justifying tears.
- Homesickness raises the status of the mailman!

C. To Answer a Question

We haven't talked about discussion of reading in this book (a book about writing), but some groups and classes do discuss questions. Try writing the question as a set of possible answers first. (You've begun, as usual, with good full pages of observations of what you're studying.) Use the subject of the question as the subject of a set of sentences. For example, let's say the question is, "What do the garden images of Marvell's poem 'The Garden' and Coleridge's 'Kubla Khan' have in common?" Write a set of sentences beginning, "In both poems the gardens...."

- In both poems the gardens have a sacred source.
- In both poems the gardens are paradises.
- Both gardens contain fountains.
- Both gardens include women figures but no actual women.
- In both poems the gardens are threatened.
- In both poems the gardens give rise to "vision" or "transcending."

Five minutes of writing like this, which is then read and heard without interruption, makes a difference. *Speech written before it's spoken differs from impulsive speech.* Discussion after even brief writing is more deliberate and more fruitful.

Double Definition: Similarity and Differences

Many are the ways of making reasonable comparisons. Writing trial sentences helps you to begin reasonably and simply, no matter what direction your comparison finally takes. The logic of comparing two things is:

> *one* basic similarity—the basis of the comparison, and one significant difference—the important way in which they differ *on the basis of the comparison.*

Two problems haunt most of the comparison/contrast essays I've ever read. They are either nothing but lists of similarities and differences, or they are unfair, the so-called "invidious comparison." The unfair comparison says one thing is good in a certain way ("This poem is full of images,") while the other thing is not good in that way ("but that poem has few images.") In other words, the invidious comparison doesn't really compare two things; it acts as the enemy to one of the things. (*Invidious* comes from the Latin *invidere*: to envy, to hate, to grudge, to hinder.) We have been helping you avoid invidious comparisons: in the *Once/Now* essay, where you made sure you had no negative on one side of the seed sentence; and in the *Two-Voices* essay, where you said how each voice was valid.

There's a simple way of using trial sentences to make a fair and fruitful comparison. Begin with plenty of written observations about the subjects of comparison. Then write 2 sets of trial sentences. Write first to find a similarity, the *one* basis for the comparison. Here are examples from a class that had been reading *Narrative of the Life of Frederick Douglass, An American Slave* and Willa Cather's *Sapphira and the Slave Girl.*

1. In both books characters are freed from slavery.
2. In both books, violence and slavery go together.
3. Both books are set in the past.
4. Both books contain narratives apart from the main story.
5. In both books religion and slavery are associated.
6. Both books have a dramatic turning point followed by a flatter ending.

Then the writer selected *one* basis for comparison. There can only be one basis for comparison, just as there is one foundation for one building. On that basis, then, the writer wrote trial sentences to find the significant difference:

1. In both books characters are freed from slavery, but in *Narrative* Frederick is freed by revolt while in *Sapphira* Nancy is freed by obedience.

2. In *Narrative* the slave analyzes slavery, but in *Sapphira* the free people analyze slavery.

3. Nancy is freed from slavery completely when she goes North, but Frederick remains involved with slavery as an Abolitionist.

4. Frederick's freedom begins with his education; Nancy's freedom begins with the education of others.

By the end of the second set of trial sentences, the writer was ready to pick what was for him the most significant difference of those he had found and to write a first paragraph to explain the idea that will organize his observations into an essay.

PART THREE

Writing about Literature

35

Why *Write* about Literature?

Most people like to talk about what they read. It's a way of being social, and they enjoy the sense that they can talk about literature with other readers. But to write about literature implies going beyond trading opinions to thinking, rereading, and putting together an idea.

When you write your own literature, you begin with a sense of the whole form—the fable shape, for example. The form draws out of your mind the experience you need to embody it. When you write about someone else's literature, reading, rereading, and observing come first. But when you're ready to write, you'll need what you needed before: a sense of the whole form (that's the shape of your essay) and experience of the literature to give your idea a body. You write easily when your reading has become experience, a knowledge of the work from the inside.

How do you get a good idea? By paying a special kind of attention to what you read: 1) You always see it as a whole, a single coherent world; 2) your perception of it increases as you keep on contemplating it; 3) you examine it personally, directly at its source; 4) you derive energy from what you perceive. So writing about literature implies reading it with a special power that comes from the literature itself.

A work of literature is its own world, ample and indivisible. It contains all the data you need to write well about it. You can't exhaust it, and it even offers you a language for writing because it's a world made out of language.

Literature's right ordering of words gives you a heightened energy. To examine the work, you use its informed energies without exhausting your own. You can read anything, fearlessly.

Why? Because literature is an ordinary and public part of human life. School books talk as if literature "enriches" our lives, but it's more realistic to say that literature is central to our psychic and emotional balance. Humans composed wise sentences, poems, drama, stories long before there was writing; and children possess yards of oral literature before they go to school or learn to read. Composing/hearing literature is so necessary to human life that it can't be confined to books.

Every educated person wants to be an expert reader; hardly anyone needs to be a critic. Literature is filled with the power of language, and our connection with that power is pleasure. So the first step is to give ourselves permission to read with pleasure. The response of pleasure leads us to the center of the work.

"But," you say, "suppose I don't like what I have to read?" Well, you don't have to like it. Pleasure isn't the same as liking, which is a matter of taste. You might not like the taste of pears, for example, but you can still sense the pleasure of a perfectly-flavored, perfectly fresh pear. Taste can't be assigned; it's the pleasure you choose for yourself. You should always read all the literature you like best, for from it you learn what no one can teach you.

Tastes are shifting, but expert readers recognize the pleasure in literature even beyond their own range of taste. Pleasure is more permanent than taste and has more mind to it: it's the human experience of the perfection of a particular thing. That perfection is the center of the literature you're studying. When you see the center, you can begin writing your essay.

36

Response

The Core Essay

Recall a fable from your group or write a new one; read it aloud. Choose one aphorism and copy it. For 2 minutes nonstop, write observations about how the sentence is written. Begin with the obvious, with what attracts you the most. Read these observations aloud to each other.

Here's a poem almost as brief as an aphorism. Read it aloud.

THE SPAN OF LIFE

The old dog barks backward without getting up.
I can remember when he was a pup.

Robert Frost

Write a copy of the poem. As you copy it, notice that you read the poem in a special, more leisurely and intense way than you usually read prose. Listen to it read again, without following the poem with your eyes. The poem you hear has different dimensions from the poem you read silently. For example, there are pauses in the poem you hear that are simply empty spaces among the printed words on the page. The silences you hear are alive like the pause between pulse beats or the rests in music.

You're reading and listening to generate attention. If you wanted information, you'd skim the text to pick up the main point. But a poem no more contains that kind of information than a sunrise does. Take the poem in as a whole, unhurriedly, as you'd watch a sunrise or listen to music.

Now write nonstop 3 minutes a list of what you noticed about how the poem is written or designed. Begin with the obvious, what attracts you most strongly. For example, I notice that the poem ends with *pup* and begins with *old dog*.

Read your observations to each other. Listen attentively, but don't interrupt them for comment.

To write about literature you need to separate observations from inferences so you won't misrepresent what you read or start talking about it in a way that leads you away from it. For example, you may imagine what a character in a story is thinking, but it makes all the difference in the world whether the author actually tells you what the character is thinking or whether the author refrains from telling you.

Reread your observations and consider what has changed between the beginning and the end of the poem. In every work of literature, no matter how short, something changes between the first line and the last. You are not where you were in the beginning; you do not see things in the same way at the end.

Write nonstop for 10 minutes an answer to this question, "What is the turning point of the poem, and why do you think so?" Write freely. There's no one right answer to this question; you can't get it wrong.

At home reread the poem and quickly write more observations about how the poem is written. Read these. Then continue your writing on the turning point question. Write nonstop for 40 minutes. This gives you a rough draft of a 50-minute essay.

New First Paragraph

You wrote your core essay by answering an elemental question, "What is the turning point and why do you think so?" You can ask this question of any literature from poetry to a book of anthropology. There's no one right answer, because a well-made book or poem is a whole: everything fits—that's the root meaning of *art* (*ar-* to fit together). In a unity the center is everywhere. You probably began by locating the turning point, saying where you see it. But if the center is everywhere, *where* you see the center depends on *how* you see it.

You see a center where the balance of the poem tips: the beginning changes into the end. Some poems seem not to turn but to go straight on. Then the center strikes you as a recognition point, where you realize how the beginning becomes the ending, how the end becomes inevitable.

Now you move from where you see the center to what it is. The elemental question helps you organize your observations into a definition.

Recall one of the core essays read in your group and have it reread. Listen, then ask the author to read it again. Write for 5 minutes nonstop a set of 5 trial sentences like this: "The poem turns from *what* to *what* (as the author of the essay sees it)?" Look over your sentences and write nonstop another set of 5 trial sentences like this: "In this essay the central idea is that...." Check your best sentences. Read these aloud to each other.

Copy your best version of your idea as the first sentence of a new paragraph. Write nonstop 4 or 5 more sentences to say more about the idea. This way of unpacking the idea into a paragraph gives you a definition of the governing idea of the essay. Read these paragraphs to each other.

Definire, the Latin word at the root of *define,* contains the word *finis,* which means boundary or limit. So the simplest sense of *define* is to draw a boundary line around your idea to show what its limits are. Your first paragraph is that boundary line. Your reader can see the shape of your whole idea in your first paragraph, and from that can recognize the idea in each of its parts as you organize your observations to support your idea in the body of your essay.

Going consciously through these steps is the road to mastering definition. Practice them again on your own essay:

- Write nonstop a set of 5 trial sentences to get at the heart of your idea: "The poem turns from *what* to *what?*" (Or, if you don't see the center as a turn, "The poem changes from *this* at the beginning to *this* by the end.")
- Write nonstop a set of 5 trial sentences: "The central idea of this essay is that..."
- Choose the best sentence. Write to say more about its idea.

Keep writing till you have 4 more sentences. This is your new first paragraph.

This is definition: pulling out of your concrete observations an idea of what they mean to you. The elemental question is a way of making your purpose in writing explicit and bringing it to bear on your thinking so far. Your new first paragraph centers on the idea and its parts. You know the poem by your own observations, but you don't discuss the details of the poem in the first paragraph. First draw the boundary line around your idea, make it recognizable, and ready yourself for another look at the way your observations will shape up as evidence.

At home write your own new first paragraph as you did with the sample essay in class. Then go on to extend your core essay by writing a new final paragraph for it, as described in Chapter 12, "The Simple Essay." The essay defined there starts with a family parable, using it as the concrete evidence part of an expository essay. The concrete part of your essay is your observations organized by the question you've been considering. Follow the directions of Chapter 12 as you extend your core essay and use the chapter as a review whenever you write a simple expository essay.

Read over what you've written. Reread the poem and your observations. Rewrite your 50-minute rough draft to give it two recognizable parts: what is the turning point; why you think so. (The two parts needn't—and probably won't—be the same length.) You needn't write an introduction to your answer or a conclusion. This is a core essay; say the most important things.

As you reread your 50-minute essay, check to see whether you've written yourself away from the poem, gone off on the subject of dogs, or old age, or memory, or whatever. Bring your writing back to the poem with the aid of observations. Use your observations to support your answers to the questions. *You want at least one recognizable observation for every point you make.*

37

The Attractive Center

Copy this poem:

NOTHING GOLD CAN STAY

Nature's first green is gold;
Her hardest hue to hold.
Her early leaf's a flower,
But only so an hour.
Then leaf subsides to leaf.
So Eden sank to grief,
So dawn goes down to day.
Nothing gold can stay.

Robert Frost

As you did before, read the poem in an active, unhurried way. The short lines, which look as though they'd move fast, move slowly when they're read aloud. Reread the poem and listen to it again. As you reread, you notice how the beginning of the poem attracts you. It's leading you into the poem, and you can see how powerful the beginning of a poem is to break through the strangeness of our first reading.

As soon as another part of the poem begins to attract you as much as those opening lines, you're beginning to know the poem from the inside.

You're ready to write observations when you can start from some center in the poem. Put the text of the poem aside and write for 2 or 3 minutes nonstop. Reread the text; then put it aside once more and write observations. You're writing about the attractive center of the poem, the part that commands your attention most strongly. Don't be surprised if you find yourself attracted by parts that baffle you. Those are just the parts where it may be easiest to write observations about how the poem is written.

I find myself, for example, attracted to those lines in the poem that challenge me to take them literally. The lines say that "green is gold," that "leaf's a flower," and that "dawn goes down...." Because these lines surprise me a little, it's easier for me to separate my observations from my inferences. My observations are about the way the language surprises me; my inferences try to explain away the surprise or reduce the poem to something I knew before I read it.

I reject these inferences and strengthen my sense of the literalness of the language. For example, "dawn goes *down* to day" surprises me because I ordinarily think of dawn as the sun coming *up*. I recall the dawns I have actually seen: the rosy-gold fire along the horizon while the sky is still a little dark. I recall that I always want that fiery gold to get more intense as the sun is about to rise; but instead, as the sky lightens, the gold seems to drop out of the sky. So the poem delights me because of the resistance I feel with the word *down*, with something I didn't know I knew. Then I notice that the two previous lines establish the pattern of *down* with the words *subsides* and *sank*.

Beginning with what you sense as the center of the poem, write what you notice about how the poem is written or designed. For example, I notice that *sank* is the only past tense in the poem. Write for 3 minutes nonstop. Work close to the words of the poem, but not close to the order of the words on the page.

Now read aloud all the observations. Encourage writers to read what they've written (*not* use notes as a springboard to talk). Listen to observations with expressions of interest, but without interrupting them for comment or discussion.

Try 10 minutes of nonstop writing about your observations and use this question to help you organize your observations: What is the turning point of the poem, and why do you think so?

At home, reread the poem and quickly write more observations till you have a good pageful. Reread all your observations and your 10-minute answer to the turning point question. Then continue your answer to the question for 50 minutes of nonstop writing.

To express your response to the feeling of the poem, speak the language of the poem. Is that different from quotation? Yes. Quotation is set off from the text of your own essay. Give yourself the pleasure of speaking the language of the poem even when you're not quoting. When you need a verb to express what's going on in the poem, for example, use *subside* or *hold* or *stay*.

If you substitute your own language for the language of the poem—using words like *beauty, innocence, youth, Mother Nature* instead of Frost's words—you'll notice that your writing circles away from the poem and that you talk more about what you know outside the poem than about the poem itself.

It's a principle of all serious writing about reading: *We can't substitute our own language for the language of the text.*

To write your essay, you have two languages: the language of response and the language of literary description. To respond to the world of the poem, speak the language of the poem. To describe how the poem is written or designed, use the language of observations. One is the poem's language; one is yours. You use the poem's language for your own response, and your own language for the art of the poem.

38

Drama

The scope of this book limits our literary assignments to poetry, but we want to show you how to use an elemental question with one other kind of literature. We'll look at drama and take a poem written like a drama for a sample. The poem is "Edward," and it comes from the 15th-century border poetry of England and Scotland. We've modernized the spelling of some words and defined the meanings of the dialect words in the margin.

EDWARD

"Why does your brand• so drop with blood,   (sword)
    Edward, Edward,
Why does your brand so drop with blood,
    And why so sad go you, O?"
"O I have killed my hawk so good,
    Mother, Mother,
O I have killed my hawk so good,
    And I had no more but he, O."

"Your hawk's blood was never so red,
    Edward, Edward,
Your hawk's blood was never so red,
    My dear son I tell thee, O."
"O I have killed my red-roan steed,
    Mother, Mother,
O I have killed my red-roan steed,
    That erst• was so fair and free, O."   (once)

"Your steed was old, and you have got more,
    Edward, Edward,
Your steed was old, and you have got more,
    Some other dule• you drie•, O."   (grief, suffer)
"O I have killed my father dear,
    Mother, Mother,
O I have killed my father dear,
    Alas, and woe is me, O!"

"And what penance will you do for that,
    Edward, Edward?
And what penance will you do for that,
    My dear son, now tell me, O?"
"I'll set my feet in yonder boat,
    Mother, Mother,
I'll set my feet in yonder boat,
    And I'll fare over the sea, O."

"And what will you do with your towers and your hall,
    Edward, Edward,
And what will you do with your towers and your hall,
    That were so fair to see, O?"
"I'll let them stand till they down fall,
    Mother, Mother,
I'll let them stand till they down fall,
    For here never more must I be, O."

"And what will you leave to your bairns° and your wife,   (children)
    Edward, Edward?
And what will you leave to your bairns and your wife,
    When you go over the sea, O?"
"The world's room, let them beg through life,
    Mother, Mother,
The world's room, let them beg through life,
    For them never more must I see, O."

"And what will you leave to your own mother dear,
    Edward, Edward?
And what will you leave to your own mother dear,
    My dear son, now tell me, O?"
"The curse of hell from me shall you bear,
    Mother, Mother,
The curse of hell from me shall you bear,
    Such counsels you gave to me, O."

    The first sign that this poem is written as a drama is that it
has speakers, and they are characters *other* than the author or his
audience. Whenever you read a poem for the first time, check it out
with these questions: Is there a speaker? Is the speaker other than
the author or his audience? If the speaker is a child, a named human
character (often identified in the title, as, for example, "The Ruined
Maid," "The Old Pensioner"), then the poem is structured like a

drama. In drama, authors seem to disappear; they don't come on stage to tell the audience what to think.

The first speaker in "Edward" is Edward's mother, and the second speaker is Edward. Read the poem aloud twice. Stop and check on whether all the members of your group agree about what counsel Edward's mother gave him for which he now curses her.

Read the poem aloud or have it read. Write nonstop for 3 minutes what you notice about how the poem is written. Read these observations aloud, and listen to them without interruption.

Drama and stories are often harder than poetry to see as fictional. That means that some readers understand them as if they were history or reports of what happened. Writing observations about this poem is a good way to renew your sense that observations are true descriptions of how the poem is written and not opinions about what "happened," as if it actually happened.

Drama differs from story and poetry because it has an audience. The audience watches the scene from a distance and can see what the characters in the drama can't see. In fact, the audience's seeing is as much a part of the drama as the actions of the characters. The teller of a story tells his listeners things they don't know. The drama audience sees and knows things the characters in the drama don't know and can't see.

When studying a drama, ask yourself which character has the purpose that starts the action going—the action you're actually watching. In "Edward," that action is asking and answering questions, and the mother starts the action going by asking the questions. Then ask yourself the special question for drama: "What does this character *not* see?"

Try this question with "Edward." Let's assume that the mother is the ignorant—the unknowing or unseeing character. That's a reasonable assumption because she's the one who asks the questions. Write for 5 minutes nonstop a set of answers to the question, "What does the mother not see?" Begin with the obvious. Read to each other your set of sentences.

Here's an example of a set of trial sentences:

- The mother doesn't see where her questions are leading.
- The mother doesn't see that Edward's gift will be a curse.
- The mother doesn't see that Edward is giving her a share of his penance.
- The mother doesn't see that Edward has already given her the fruit of her counsels.

At home, reread your observations and your set of sentences. Write more observations till you have a good pageful. Begin your observations with the attractive center of the poem. This practice is especially important for plays and novels which are too long for you simply to follow the reading order.

With your observations and your answers to the drama question in mind, write your answer to the elemental question, "What is the turning point, and why do you think so?"

Compose the second stage of this essay as you did before.

39

A Look at the Whole

Your essay analyzing what you read, like your other expository essays, supports the idea it asserts. Your best evidence comes from your observations, the public and recognizable part of your thinking. Your idea defines how one expert reader (you) sees the art of the poem (or any other work) and why you see it that way.

"But," you say, "what if my observations are wrong? What if I've got the wrong turning point? What if my responses are wrong, or I have the wrong center, or am working on an unimportant part of what I read?" None of these things can be wrong. In literature there are no wrong parts, no unimportant parts, no false centers. You can depend on the unity of the work you read.

You bring your whole self to your reading. Your identity is the personal source of your observations, just as the unity of the work is the literary source of your observations. You don't have to know all about your self to have confidence in your powers, any more than you have to know all about the work of literature. Identity is wider and deeper than our consciousness of it.

Here's a summary of what we have been saying about studying and writing about literature:

- Find and work with the attractive center of what you read. This implies that you encourage yourself to read with pleasure and that you pay attention to your own response as well as to what you read.
- Enjoy the baffling or puzzling parts of what you read. They make it easy to locate the new things you learn from the work, and they are the easiest to write observations about. There is no need to translate them.
- You have two "languages" for writing your essay: the language of response, which is the language of the work itself, and the language of literary description—written observations. Expert readers speak the language of the work freely, just as expert travelers speak the language of the country in which they travel. It's not "plagiarism" to speak the language of the work any more than it's plagiarism to speak French in Paris.
- Separate observations from inferences. Your mind both observes and draws inferences from what it notices; but obser-

vations describe the literature, while inferences reveal what you think about the literature. You want to be clear about the differences, because observations are evidence for your assertions, but inferences are not. Observations are usually about the way the language of the work surprises you.

• Study and examine by writing. Write your observations. Write 4 or 5 versions of your key idea. Write trial sentences defining your idea. If you separate thinking from writing, it will be difficult later to express your thinking *in* writing.

• If you sense a problem, look again at the way the work is written or designed. What baffles you may be meant as a baffle; perhaps the work can't be confronted or broken into. Slide around and find a welcome at the side door or an open window. Read the work in the most elemental way. Nothing outside the literature explains difficulties or solves problems as well as finding more ways in which its parts refer to each other. The center is everywhere.

40

Analysis

Teachers outside writing classes expect you to have the skills of analysis confidently in place. Since the writing skills you have now are suitable and sufficient for analysis, it's time to consider it.

You've concentrated on writing literature, starting with your sense of a whole shape: fable, parable, essay. You generated your material by imagining its form. When you rewrote, you gave your writing an analytic turn by pulling an idea out of it, defining the idea, and putting the definition up front. The question form of each of the six essay shapes gave you a way of analyzing each shape.

It's going to be easy for you to imagine writing an extended analysis now because you've been through the form. In fact, you've written brief analyses in the section you've just finished, "Writing About Literature."

Analysis is really a refinement of the pleasure of paying attention. We can sort out how it works just as we did with the idea of grammar—to dissipate the dismay the word *analysis* sometimes stirs up. Grammars are based on something universally human: the power to generate language; and analysis springs out of a human power, too: the way we catch sight of the shapes that work behind the appearances of things. It's as ordinary as watching children run and jump, and finally realizing it's a game they're playing. More watching and we intuit the game-ground and the rules. A little more thinking and we figure out how such games are lost and won.

Analysis is recognizable in simple ways, and once you recognize it you'll know you've done it and can do it.

What It Is

Analysis is a way of finding a set of elemental parts in a body of material. Once you've found the set, you can test the material or reorder its parts to use it in a new way.

Socrates analyzed ideas by means of dialogue: asking his acquaintances questions and then questioning their answers. But the practice of analysis really emerged and spread with the development of writing and printing. Analysis depends on writing because it's done in two operations. The first, thinking operation is searching, is unformulated; so it's not easy to remember without being written down. The second operation is decisive: it shapes the end—and, of course, writing is the best shaper.

Recognizing Analysis

Analysis is so individual and various that it would be wrong to limit it to one definition. But all analysis has certain marks. You can recognize it in its purpose and in its method.

Analysis comes from two Greek parts: *ana-lysis*, meaning *up-loosening*, literally. In Greek, the word is used to mean loosening bonds, opening the mouth, releasing captives on receipt of ransom, unyoking teams, and bending the bow. These are metaphors for the work of analysis when it solves problems. And that is one of its purposes. It unties knots, flexes tension. and separates yoked parts. Analysis also clarifies the knowledge we already have, and that's its great purpose in schools.

The method of analysis is a way of thinking, and it goes, as we said, in two operations. First it gathers materials by observing data. Then, by means of a question or purpose, the analyzer pulls the materials through a second operation: ordering them as a *set* of elements that work together, a structure.

The thinking-writing of the first stage of analysis goes in a certain order: from observations of data to a set. The shaping-writing of the second stage of analysis reverses the order of the first stage: it begins with the set (the idea) and then presents the observations as evidence or support for the idea.

Analytic writing is the opposite of narrative writing. In a detective story, the author builds *toward* the climax and saves the solution for the end to keep the reader in suspense. If the suspense makes the reader miss a few clues, so much the better for the detective's solution. But in analytic writing, the author presents the solution first (works *away from* the climax), in order to remove suspense and free the reader's mind for paying attention to the evidence which follows. As you can see, the rules of evidence are a little stricter in real analysis than they are in detective fiction

To summarize: The purposes of analysis are to clarify knowledge and to solve problems. The method of analysis is to work in two stages: one searching and thinking, one shaping and defining. The order of the searching stage is from observation to idea (the set); the order of the defining stage is from idea to evidence (made out of observations).

What You Already Know

Your essays already show some of the marks of analysis. You compose them in two stages. The first stage is mostly concrete: experience, direct knowledge, observations, and moves toward idea.

The second stage pulls out the idea, defines it, and puts it up front as a new first paragraph.

Among the elemental skills you've been exercising, two are particularly useful for analysis: making observations and rewriting. Rewriting proliferates into practices that are simultaneously literary and analytic, especially rewriting single sentences. For example: rewriting seed sentences, turning seed sentences into elemental test questions, trial sentences, sentences that divide or double an idea. Observations teach you to reread, to search and re-search, to begin with the central, and to wake up to the form and shape of things.

What is the difference between the literature you've written and analytical writing? Literature—for example, the fable—begins with a structure (animal dialogue, ending with a moral) and embodies it, gives it the appearance of life. Thus, literature heads toward the concrete pole of writing. Analytic writing works on a whole body of concrete material by detaching a structure from it. It heads toward the abstract pole of writing. In other words, literature begins with an idea and embodies it; analysis begins with a body and makes an idea out of it.

The Whole Set

The crux of analysis is the whole set. To call it a whole set is really to say the same thing twice: a set *is* whole by definition. But it makes us more comfortable to emphasize the wholeness because the integrity of the set gives analysis its special characteristic: its dynamism.

The parts of a whole set fit together and they need each other. To omit a part or to include the wrong part is like trying to build a combustion engine without pistons or with a water wheel instead of a carburetor. You might be able to do it, but you'll never get it on the road.

But when you have a true set, it's beautiful. It gets to work right away, keeps on working, and never stops working. Set members differ and they interplay.

How do you discover such a set? Essentially, you don't discover it; you compose it. That's where individual power and point of view come in. Mental analysis is not at all like a routine chemical breakdown of water into oxygen and hydrogen. It's individual, goes deeply into personal style. The neater, the more economical an analysis is, the more flair and class it has.

If analysis is personal, does that mean we can't help you with it? If analysis were entirely a matter of thinking, we could do no more, for thinking cannot be taught. But if writing can develop the power of analysis, then that power is within your reach. Let's look at the situation again.

If our recognition marks of analysis are right and if they are a set, then by the principle of the set, you can write analysis. Since you already have skills for some of the operations, you can come into the whole set. Let's look at the idea of synthesis.

Synthesis

The set is a synthesis. That means it's an action: making, composing, putting together. It's not just out there like a lake on a mountain top. The synthesis can't be taken for granted like a mountain lake, because it's not perceivable till you make it. Back of the making is seeing. *You* see the possibility of putting observations and data together in an order that means something. But until you observe and order, no one else will dream there's anything there.

What's the difference between your parable writing and your synthesis? A good parable is like life, and its readers believe it. A good analysis is like reason, and its readers question it. The reader of a parable cannot examine its material; the reader of a scientific article or a book criticism can and will examine its material evidence.

What we call "analysis" has a double way of working. Part of it is observation or examination of nature, of events, of books. *What* you examine is out there, but your examination is not. The book is out there, but not your reading of it. No one can see your reading simply by reading the book himself. So the second and crucial part of "analysis" is synthesis: the putting of your examination together so that others can see it too.

Can you simply make a record of your examination? No—no more than you can hand in your work sheets or your lists of observations. Synthesis is not mechanical—not just a process. Synthesis is an ordering; purpose and examination are knit together at every move. That's why even a finished analysis is dynamic. It's mind in play, so double-powered that people always compare it to dialogue.

You can glimpse traces of a process in the analyzer's work sheets. The writing dissolves into crossings-out and new starts. Subjects of what might be sentences disappear, and verbs keep changing. Organization seems to be coming back with charts, diagrams, arrows pointing to words circled and underlined. But it's not yet ordered, not yet written. Even if it looks written, there are interlinings and overwritings. Jeremy Bentham, the great analyzer of English law, simply wrote his second, third, and fourth drafts right on top of the first draft. While it remained process, only he could see the order within it. A glance at such work sheets shows how analyzing— or even the composing process—and the synthesis of analysis to present it to others are not simultaneous operations.

Analysis-Synthesis → Essay

In your analysis essay you present a set of elements to your reader as a visible ordering of a reasoning concern.

1. The structure of your analysis is abstract. That means it has *reduced* the material you were examining to two or three big parts. Analysis simplifies our attention. It makes a topography out of a landscape.
2. You've pulled the structure from the concrete, the whole field of facts, identities: "the wide arable field of events" (to use Keats' phrase), everything that you can observe. You need *plenty* of observations. You kept returning to the field to write more observations.

You worked then between two poles: the need for a simple structure with few parts, and plentiful observations.

You made your synthesis, drew the map of your field, by going back and forth between these poles: plenty of observations, looking for a pattern, checking out the pattern with more observations, clarifying the pattern and fleshing it out at the same time.

Instead of flowing like literary writing, analysis proceeds by knots. In analysis, nothing is better than discovering a little snarl or patch of unbearable tension. That discovery locates the work necessary to dissolve the problem into its solution. For the same reason, you don't simply throw away observations to achieve a simple structure. By going back and forth you condense many observations into a richer one; you coordinate and subordinate into a higher order. You open one, densely-packed observation into its implications to reach a more articulated order.

It *is* a dialogue. We build analysis as Socrates did: by questioning, trying, picking our way down a path marked by knots of disagreement and the narrow agreement of two opposing voices, an abstract, reductive voice and a concrete, prolific voice, a path along which energy and concern from both sides can be kept charged and exchanged.

To accomplish your analysis you had a purpose: a problem to solve, knowledge to clarify. To write your analytical essay you had something extra: concern. All writing is literary creation. Analysis is the *re*-organizer; it can't bring the body to life. It's concern that brings writing to life as literature.

Why We Do It

This sounds like a fair amount of work—and it is, depending on your turn of mind and your degree of experience. What keeps people doing it is the pleasure of discovery, of clarifying, of solving problems. For some temperaments, it's a drama of despair and thrills: mounds of scrap paper, worn-out pencils, and midnight oil. Others do it like long-distance runners: quietly, steadily, with an unwavering passion.

Analysis, it's been said, clarifies rather than increases knowledge. That's why it's at the center of schools: to consolidate the exploring, pioneering part of learning.

If there's a literary pole of writing, where completeness and finish are important, and an analytical pole of writing, where loosening and process are important, then we've described one pole of writing in this section. It's hard to stop the process part of writing, especially for those who love analysis. That's where writing essays comes in, along with the assignments, test questions, and deadlines of schools. These limits tell you, "Throw a bounding line around it now; write it down so it will mean something." And that sends you back to the other pleasure, the literary pole of writing.

41

You Can't Do It Wrong

We keep on saying, "You can't do it wrong." You wonder how we can mean that.

"Suppose," you say, "I write stories instead of essays. Isn't that wrong? Suppose my two-part essay doesn't have two parts? What if I follow the reading order of the work in my essay about literature? And suppose I can't help saving my idea for a surprise in my last paragraph? There are a hundred ways of going wrong!"

You'd think so. But in fact, there are only a few stops short of a goal you can see. It's ways of doing essays right that are infinite.

"Why don't you give me more directions for revising and correcting?"

We give you elements. That passes the initiative to you. Elements contain their own building power, and it's greater than any directions.

"But a few instructions wouldn't hurt me."

They might. Whenever instructions are specified and detailed, they become tests.

"How can instructions become tests?"

One way of recognizing a test is to see whether you can do it wrong. An assigned procedure that can produce errors is a test. A set of actions that produces goals and ways of reaching them is learning.

"What's wrong with tests?"

Nothing. In fact that's why you're writing your essay, so you can test what you assert. But tests other people give you should come after you've learned, don't you think?

"Yes, but I'm used to learning by finding out what I do wrong and then correcting it. It makes me feel like I'm getting somewhere."

Then do it. It's useful.

"I want you to tell me my mistakes."

I wonder why I won't do that?

"I know. You want me to do it for myself."

Criticism is valuable. You should have a chance to practice it where you have most authority—on your own writing.

"Anyway, I can tell by the observations when it's not so good."

Or could be better. There's more in your mind to get onto the page. And correction at this stage really interferes with writing as it's being generated.

"What if I can't take it any further?"

Most people don't stop short of a goal they can see. When you reread the part where you sense your idea most strongly, you can probably say more about it.

"You think if I don't quit, I'll get something out of my mind."

Most people fail by quitting. Did you know that?

"If I keep writing, I can't do it wrong?"

I don't see how. Powers perfect themselves through use.

"And you don't care about misspelling?"

You care about misspelling on your essay. You want the product to look good. But don't let the product overwhelm the powers.

"You really mean it—the essay can't be wrong?"

That's right. What you've imagined in writing can't turn out to be wrong while someone else's essay is right. All the essays are right.

PART FOUR

Sample Essays

1

A Family Parable

(Chapter 10)

This is a story that my father always told us:

"When I was a teenager, we lived out in the country. If we wanted to go to town, we had to walk or go on horseback. But we only had one horse, and every time we asked our father for the horse, he always replied that it was better for us to walk because we were young and walking was good exercise for us. He always used this excuse for not lending us his horse. He rarely rode his horse, but he did not want to see anybody riding it either.

"Then I bought my first car. It was falling apart, but I could not afford a better one, and it worked even though I had trouble starting it sometimes. I will never forget it. My father was away from home at the time I bought the car. I decided to surprise him and meet him with the car. I knew that he expected me to carry his luggage all the way home. The town was quite far. My mother did not want me to drive to town. I had driven the car once before but was not a very confident driver. My mother was also afraid of what my father would say when he saw the car. He was very strict, but as long as we obeyed him we were not punished. Mother wanted me to walk to the bus station, but I wanted to show off my new car, and off I went. When my father arrived and saw the car, I was astonished he was not angry; instead he seemed rather pleased and happy. I told him I was not a very good driver yet. He said he would be only too pleased to show me how to drive. That really surprised me. As far as I knew, my father had never driven a car before, and he didn't learn in the week he was away.

"By the time we got home, I wished I had walked to town. He destroyed the car completely. He drove worse than a drunken driver. He did not know how to drive. It was years before he drove again. Whenever the subject was mentioned, he used to reply, 'The motor car will never replace the horse.' "

José Urena

Observations

1. You sense that the story is going to be some sort of turnabout, but it's hard to see how. Father's spoken of by the narrator and the mother. He doesn't actually appear till the last moment in the story, and by then we're eager to see how he acts.

He's a recognizable type: the strict father. We see him through the eyes of the child who's less powerful, yet sees through the father's "reason": that walking is good for children. This insight prepares us for the narrator's initiative in buying a car and in driving it to pick up the father. The pretense or imposition in the father's character, seen in his pronouncement about the horse, prepares us for his imposing on his son by showing him "how to drive." The reversal is partly for the father, his unreasonableness exposed, but also partly for the son who wishes after all that he'd walked to the station. Their purposes have crossed, but not in ways anyone foresaw.

Father has the last word (most of the words are his) and the word is typical, but this time his words undercut him even more: a personal assertion pronounced as if it were a general truth. The son, recognizing a no-win situation, *lets* him have the last word.

2. The dry recollection of the big moment when father gets off the bus centers the story. "That really surprised me" and "He didn't learn in the week he was away" are fairly strong statements but in the context vastly understated and funny. From the center come the consequences—the end of the son's dilapidated car, the father's driving, and the likelihood of the father's making further claims to omnicompetence. Perhaps there's also an end to the son's ability to hear such claims with a straight face, but it's the genius of this story to refrain from saying so. It ends instead by giving the father one more chance to make an assertion—and this time the reader as well as the writer know it's preposterous.

The way into the center is via descriptions of the father's attitude toward his horse and his obedient children, of the mother's sense of the father's authority, of the son's reflections on these.

At the beginning the son sees through the father's excuse for exclusive claim to the horse, but the father stays serenely in command. (In between is the small surprise of the son's using father's absence to buy a car.) At the end the son shows he knows how to limit his own claims to power—he admits he is "not a very good driver yet"— while father and son both know by experience what neither now need say: that the father's unlimited claims are insubstantial. What the mother knows about both of them isn't stated, but we may suspect she sees more than she speaks of.

2

Simple Essay (Chapter 12)

Sorrowness or grief is the pain of the mind. If it comes by the loss of a loved person it is loss of a happiness which was a large part of life. The death of a very close relative is very painful. Memory keeps bringing back images because of the potent influence that person had in our life. The death of a loved relative means that our lives have changed completely to let grief in.

My grandmother was my favorite human being. The only time I ever saw her cry was when grandpa died. Tiny and hunched over in her black widow's dress, she wept for the man she had shared her life with, for almost fifty years. It had been a hard life, but grandma never complained. She was not much more than five feet tall, but she was strong and wiry. She cleaned other people's houses for many years, but still she found time to cook and bake for us. Her coal-black eyes usually twinkled with laughter. When I did not mind my own manners, though, those eyes could blaze with anger. But she never stayed mad for long. After a few minutes, she would hand me a fresh-baked cookie or tell me about some stunt she pulled in her own childhood.

Her voice was much louder than you would expect for such a little lady. Many times she made me jump when she shouted loudly my name. She could also be gentle and tender. Her hands were rough and hard from years of hard work, but they were soft whenever they touched me. When she died at the age of seventy-five, she was buried next to my grandfather. That was her last wish. I have missed her every day since. Sometimes, when I am alone, I think about my grandmother and see her in my imagination. She is standing in front of me mending my clothes while I play with a little car on the floor. She is always working and never seems to be overcome by weariness. I will never forget her as long as I live.

Death is something we will have to face some day. When we lose someone we love by death, we should accept it courageously in our grief. We can think about how lucky we are to have had this person in our life. We can imagine how good they have been, and say that we are fortunate to have known them. The grief will pass but the memory will stay.

José Urena

Observations

1. The central image is in the present tense: she is mending my clothes; I am playing with a little car. It's not a memory of direct engagement, not even one of special happiness for the child. It's memory of ordinary repeated actions.

I like the ordinariness of it because it suggests the habitual, the peaceful part of life. His grandmother's presence was part of the life he didn't have to be conscious of because nothing interrupted it—especially death.

His loss and grief is mirrored within the example by his grandmother's grief for her husband.

His memories show how grown-up consciousness works back into childhood memories: she cooked good things for him. Now he sees she did so over and above a life of hard work. There are some concrete images—black snapping eyes and small stature—but these are tied to actions which show her character and values: she wanted him to mind his manners; she worked hard. I like the way he says sorrows *open up* our lives to let grief in because *open* suggests not just loss but expansion of sympathy and consciousness. He asserts that grief is not easy to get over, though we know feelings become less sharp in time. But the way his grandmother's image persists both in relation to him and in her own feelings and character shows grief having a lasting effect on thought.

2. The definition of "sorrowness," grief, echoes off other abstract words around it: memory, happiness, loss, life, influence. The center too has many such words in among its snapshots from memory: angry, always, gentle, tender. The snapshots—a small lady with bright dark eyes, high-tempered, full of feeling, expressive, watching the boy with his home-baked cookie or his little car—come into one stream of thought made by the emotional current of all the words in the essay. The memories are extraordinary not in themselves but in their sharp glimpses of how much meaning ordinary days can convey. The speaker shows up not so much in self-description but in this poignantly conveyed point of view: the needs of grief sharpen his focus on the lost grandmother. Not he but his grief is present. I notice, in "sorrowness," the special power often shown in ESL writing—what is in one sense a mistake in another makes a word shine with new light for native speakers.

The address of this essay is as much to the author's self as to us—he's committing the experience of loss to memory as well as to paper. We hear and we overhear him.

3

Writer's Proof
Essay on an Assigned Topic (Chapter 19)

REPRESSION

To live a life repressed, unable to fulfill dreams or retain inborn pride, can lead to one of two states: the repressed continue their goose-step gait, each step digging deeper into submission; or they reach beyond their restricted terrain into the hidden corners of their minds, where blind hope rules, and form plans of rebellion for recovering lost desires. We are born with neither knowledge of the past nor insight into the future. Circumstance dictates to us our options.

The year was 1920. A war was over. Prohibition swept its ruling hands over the stills and whiskey joints of the country. Anger streamed through many. The medicine for their illness was being pried and pulled from them. Their illness was life and the cold truths it brought. For the immigrants one of these truths, these awakening realizations, was that the streets of America weren't paved with gold, but they were instead paved with cracked cobblestones that broke their hurried stride, unbalanced their gait, and tripped them making them fall and scratch their knees. Alcohol could soothe these wounds and any others.

Prohibition wasn't a deterrent of drinking. It was merely an inconvenience to those who drank and a profitable convenience for those who didn't. My great-grandfather arrived here with the clouded idea that opportunities would be showered on him. Being struck by the fact that his honest ambition wasn't enough, he seized the circumstance. He and his wife began bootlegging whiskey in their back room. They remained indoors, hidden with their illegal secret. But my grandfather had to publicly acknowledge it, for each day he was sent to the bottle manufacturer to get the daily supply of whiskey bottles. As he walked home with twenty pounds of bottle slung over his back in a burlap sack, he was accompanied by the music the bottles made. Clang, clang, they knocked together, announcing to the world his secret.

"Bottles! Bottles!" the children yelled. "We know what you do! Bottles, bottles!"

It wasn't worth it, he thought. It wasn't worth the ten cents his parents gave him. It wasn't worth the movies he could see or the ice cream he could buy with the money.

Kids were kids and kids were mean. They teased everyone. But that didn't ease his shame. For my grandfather Prohibition held none of the romance that spices up novels about that era. He saw no speakeasies and he never met Al Capone.

He walked at last down the tenement steps empty handed.

"Bottles! Bottles!"

His appearance alone signalled the chant.

"Bottles! Bottles!" they yelled as he skipped down the cobble-stones toward the factory.

It is now 1945. Another war is over and the government's hands are resting.

My father is riding his bicyle. Clang! Clang! His bicycle made a racket as it bumped along the street. He was on his way home from his job at the local liquor store where he was a delivery boy. He was really too young to work there, but he was cheaper than an older boy and the owner saw no harm in that.

His bicycle was built of stray parts he'd found in a junk yard. The wheels didn't match in size, and most of the parts were rusted. He had asked his father for money to buy a bicycle, promising to repay him with his first paycheck. But his father refused, unwilling to part with his money even temporarily.

Clang! Clang! The bicycle jumped, scratched and screeched along.

"Clang! Clang!" the children yelled. "Here comes Johnny with his junk-yard bike! Clang! Clang!"

It hurt a bit to have the kids tease him, but it was worth it. He had change in his pocket; he could go to the movies and buy ice cream. At ten years old he was someone. His ambition didn't come from hearsay dreams. He knew the streets weren't paved with gold, but they weren't paved with cobblestones either. They were paved with smooth cement which made riding his bicycle easier.

We are, as the familiar quote states, victims of circumstance. But we are hopeful, cunning, resourceful, and fiercely proud victims who reflect the triumphs and imperfections of the present ruling hand. The governments of the world can be seen as ropes and we as the objects they tie. A rope coiled too tightly about an object can injure it and is sure to unravel. But a cord, tied looser, will still secure an object; all that is changed is the likelihood of injury. We, the damaged goods of society, draw from the circumstance what we can, moving about in the space our rope leaves us and at times even unravelling it.

Diane Sirotnak

4

Writer's Proof
Essay on an Assigned Quotation
(Chapter 20)

"The great thing in all education is to make our nervous system our ally instead of our enemy.... We must make automatic and habitual, as early as possible, as many useful actions as we can."

Since habits train our nervous systems to contribute to our education, I agree that we should form good habits early. Habits are actions that we do not have to stop and think about. They save us trouble.

One habit which I now have is a very useful action. I get up early every single morning. People are surprised when I say I get up at 6:30 every day because I like to. I am on my way before the other people in my house get up.

I used to sleep late all the time, especially on school days. I turned the alarm off in my sleep, and my mother had to wake me at least three times before I could get out of bed. Then I would have the trouble of rushing or being late.

When I was ten years old, my father got me a beautiful surprise for a birthday gift. It was a real live puppy. He was a mixed breed. My mother called him a mongrel, and she wasn't too happy with this new member of the household. She wouldn't let me have him unless only I was responsible. I would be responsible to train him and get him housebroken. She told me all the work I would have to do. It sounded as if I could do it, so I said, "Let me try."

My parents gave me a book on feeding and caring for a dog. I also got a book out of the library. Training a dog to be housebroken is much different than in the books. It seems I was always mopping up puddles. Everybody gave me hints. My friends and I gave him a name, George, which was the first name of the principal of our school. We thought it was funny when we said, "Here, George," and, "No, no George." He learned his name very well. But when I wasn't watching him he chewed up shoes, magazines, and toy cars instead of his rawhide ball I bought him.

After one month I thought it would take forever. He could let me know he wanted out, but always too late. I realized that if he was just out in the yard fast enough in the morning he'd be all right, no puddles in the house. Also he would not have a chance to chew on my books or my brother's toys. I took him out earlier and earlier in the morning. After that, it didn't take him too long to be house-broken all the time.

I still take George for a walk every morning. No matter if I was out late the night before, I still get up at 6:30. I have a clock-radio alarm clock, but I don't need it. I get up before it starts playing. I like the streets with no cars going. George keeps me company and I feel safe.

Getting up early is a habit I got as soon as possible. I was doing it so I could train George. But also I was doing it for myself. George trained me to get up and use the morning. Looking back on it, I wish I had many good habits I trained myself in at such an early age.

Marta Goldman

5

"They Say" (Chapter 26)

JUST A MOTHER

They say, "It doesn't take much to be a mother. Any simple-minded female, who is biologically equipped can be one." They say that a man is far too busy with the important business of bread winning to raise children. They reason that men simply do not have the patience to deal with spills, spats, and tears; and they think that women do. They suspect that all really good middle-class mothers stay at home with their children, tending to their needs, which *they* never clearly define.

Only the surface of motherhood is seen until you actually enter in. You think you know beforehand how you'll have to clean and care for your child, but it all seems easy enough.

Before I had children, I did what they call work. My jobs varied but in a word they were all tedious, and in two words they were tedious and dull. For the most part I did sales and clerical work. Narrow-mindedly, I thought that any and all other jobs would be equally as dull. There was a longing within me for something more than answering phones and pouring coffee.

I decided to have a family. I knew beforetime that I'd be the kind of mother who stayed home with her children, like *they* say you should. After all who wanted to work anyway? They say women don't work, meaning housewives don't work: well, that suited me fine.

The unspeakable joy I felt when I found out I was pregnant was accentuated by the relief I felt at the thought of never having to work again. From all they said about motherhood I figured I knew a lot. Judging by its title alone "just motherhood" sounded pretty easy.

They say things like there are no bad children, only bad mothers: and good mothers have happy babies. Since I aimed to be a very good mother I anticipated having a happy baby.

When my baby finally arrived I nursed her. Enjoying every moment, I'd hold and hug her. I couldn't understand why she cried so much. As a matter of fact she seemed to cry every time I put her down. Partly because I thought something was hurting her and partly from sheer exhaustion I started to cry with her: realizing all too soon that this being just a mother was not as easy as they had led me to believe. Here I was at the beck and call of this little one who indeed had stolen my heart, and I didn't know what to do!

It was a hard time during which I questioned my ability: "Could it be that I haven't the patience that they say mothers have?" I wondered. Instead of patience being something I had, I realized how much I needed it. My experience has shown me that patience is not inborn. Perhaps you could say it is something that one acquires; but I think that is misleading because it suggests permanence. My patience was born out of love for my family and a deep desire that I had to be what they needed me to be. Still though, after ten years of experience, patience sometimes without even notifying me, just flees from my side. There I'll stand yelling, realizing that with patience I could be making my point much more effectively. Well, why do you lose your patience? you might ask. Sometimes it seems like it happens over the silliest things, like a milk spill, or a spat between two of the children, but it goes deeper.

It's the fact that motherhood is a job. It's a job that entails the awesome responsibility for the lives of others. It's not easy as it has been said to be. It's unending work. As a mother, I work from 7 in the morning until 10 at night. Though I eat, I do so on the job. As children get older you do get breaks, but when they're babies forget it! Sometimes you don't even get a good night's sleep. Add one sleepless night to one day of cleaning, washing, feeding, etc. and you've got one tired mother. I've learned that when I'm tired I can neglect to show my love for my children. I know this is human but I also know that the effect of neglecting (for whatever the reason) to show love to our children can be devastating.

Our reactions to them are so important. Whether we're tired or angry, happy or sad, they're first. For many years their only concern is how we treat them. I've learned that children are egocentric. They need to be taught to think of others without being made to feel guilty about their own inclinations toward self: guilt over their nature can rob them of their self-esteem. So my experience as a mother has shown me that we have to love our children unconditionally while teaching them right from wrong. If that sounds easy it's not; at least, not as an on-going thing.

I've learned that mothers often have to put their feelings aside for the sake of their children. The way we treat our children determines, to a great extent, how they will be as adults. And that is very important, not only for children and mothers but to the whole world: children are its future.

So when I hear them say, "Oh, she's just a mother" or "I'm tired of working: I want to stay home and be just a mother", I think, "Oh, Oh! they really don't know what they're talking about. God help them."

Joanne Nizzo

Observations

1. The essay goes through three stages: what "they" say and she thought too, the drastic contrast with experience, and a general part about the idea of mothering. This last even extends to the condition of being a child, and so brings the essay round to its beginning when she was little more than a child.

I loved the ironies, especially the big one that brings together her "unspeakable joy" at being pregnant with the relief she felt at "never having to work again."

There are several stages of what "they" say and they mark every stage of her developing experience: mothers, babies, patience. This keeps illustrating her early statement that only the surface of motherhood is seen until you really enter in. The essay is the stages of her entering in to a bigger and bigger experience until she sees it expand beyond her own experience of it.

She keeps the big words, like *patience*, right together with concrete, ordinary language, like "stand there yelling."

Most remarkable to me is how she sees and accepts the young child's "natural" self-centeredness and sees the parents' job as teaching right from wrong, but separating it from guilt. It's also "natural" to "stand there yelling." She takes herself past her weakness by seeing the value of her social role, and in the same way she takes the children past their weakness by defining their value to society.

"*Awesome* responsibility" goes nicely with "*God* help them!"

2. The turn is delicious as Joanne moves from fantasy to reality, listening to a baby cry though she has done everything she'd believed necessary. It's her first day of school as the baby begins to educate her.

She begins with the notion of women and babies and even joins those who say them, assuming that the name "mother" sounds like an easy job-title. By the end she speaks after years of mothering young children.

She does not want children to be selfish, but does not want to reproach them for their natural self-esteem. In this part she tacitly forgives herself. That done she can look out to young women with notions of babies yet unborn and wish them well, God help them.

It's a story of ignorance overcome by action, undaunted by local failure or temporary guilt. Her ignorance is diminished by dailiness and replaced by experiential knowledge.

6

Two Voices (Chapter 28)

THERE'S NO PLACE LIKE HOME

It hasn't been quiet in my home for a long, long time, and it probably never will be again. For as long as I can remember, my family has been divided into two warring factions, the sleepers and the non-sleepers, and though it may seem trivial to some, it has caused a great deal of unrest in my family.

A sleeper is a person who wakes up at noon, lounges until one, and usually stumbles in around three in the morning. Whereas, a non-sleeper, or to be more specific, the early riser, is one who naturally gets up early, usually when the sun rises, and plunges into the day's work. Because of the large number of people in my family, nine to be exact, this problem at times has reached epic proportions. The sides are divided evenly with a parent in each corner, and the only uninvolved parties are our dog and cat.

My mother, brother Joey, sisters Barbara and Maureen are all sleepers. They love waking up to the noon sun shining in their windows. They lie there for a long while just enjoying the peace, soaking up all the energy before they begin their day. They enjoy the lazy weekends and dread the Monday morning alarm. It is important that they get that extra sleep in the morning, or the entire day is shot, leaving them tired and irritable. Often my sister Barbara sets her alarm an hour before, so she can get used to the idea of getting up. The problem is there are other people in our home who are not relaxing in bed. My father usually decides to vacuum at 7:00 in the morning, and the roar of the vacuum cleaner undoubtedly wakes the others up. If it is not the vacuum cleaner, it is the radio or hair dryer or the rattling of pots and pans that forces the sleeper into consciousness. When a sleeper is waked up, invariably an argument starts, so anyone who is not up by then soon will be, and the war begins.

On the other hand, the early risers: my father, sisters Mary and Patty, and my brother Anthony, wake with ease. Without the aid of an alarm clock, they begin the day with the one hundred and one things that need to be done, such as: washing, dressing, cleaning, shopping, and cooking. They couldn't stay in bed if they wanted to.

It's as if the morning is drawing them up and out of bed into a higher energy level. They are cheerful and industrious in the morning. Often they cook elaborate breakfasts for everyone and serve as human alarm clocks for the rest of the sleeping household. It seems as though they get everything going in the morning which, in turn, makes everything easier for the others. From their point of view, it is difficult to be quiet while you are cleaning, and it simply is not fair to ask them to wait until everyone's up. It is a waste of time for them, especially when one of my sisters is always falling asleep on the couch in front of the television. Why should they be penalized for someone else's habits? It's not as if they don't try, but how quiet can you be? Waking someone up is unavoidable. They feel it's their rights that are being infringed upon, not the sleepers'.

This war is sure to go on indefinitely with neither side the victor, because there will always be those who like to sleep late and those who do not. Neither side is right or wrong, good or bad. They have different biological time clocks which more than likely will never change.

Elizabeth Drew

Observations

1. Elizabeth promises us an epic version of irreducible conflict, and makes her mock epic work. There's even a mini-catalogue listing sleepers-in, matched by a later catalogue of deeds done by wakers-up. We get the noises of the risen and the satisfying stirrings of the prone.

I like the busyness of it all—even the sleepers are shown in action, just one mediating figure who is willingly awake but somnolent an hour ahead of her rising time. It's a big interactive family, with troops like mother, drowsy in the morning, and troops like father, vacuuming at 7 A.M. With so many little parts she yet avoids letting her tale be mere listing. Every character has something to do, something which is telling. The sense of outrage each side feels for the behavior of the other is kept not only in balance but light, jovial, the opposite of murderous. Each group means well and acts for the best.

The author is the stand and pivot of the balance, uncommitted to either side, sustaining the arguments of each side equally. Keeping out of the argument lets her consider with affectionate irony the merits she doesn't assert from any point of view of her own. Her own dry wit finally does run out of reasonableness, so to conclude she reaches to our country's answer in every dilemma: science. She gets help and justification for her noncommital tone by referring it all to nature, something void of ill will, determined and unchangeable, the biological clock no one can avoid having or change.

2. Both sides are developed amply. While I heard one side, I fell into full sympathy with it and was surprised to find, later, that there's another view of the situation. It's like the fun of reading Browning or Shaw and watching them coolly make the unmakable case.

The complete division of the household, with only the animals excepted, makes the situation seem a universal human condition. Her language also enlarges the situation, to make it more absurd: *epic, war, biological, always will be.*

Each side almost seems to be speaking, though they're not quoted, because the author speaks their language: "important to get that extra sleep," vs. "makes everything easier for the others." Each side sees itself as the center, and the narrator lets them make their claims. It's wonderful how much good language each side finds for itself when you think how each might be described. The early risers are not noisy busy-bodies, but "cheerful and industrious," doing the "101 things that need to be done." The late risers aren't lazy louts, but enjoyers of peace, "soaking up energy." Both sides are associated with the sun by the narrator's language: the sleepers soaking up the noon sun, lying in bed as if *they* were truly in harmony with the day; and the early risers being drawn up out of bed by the morning to a higher energy level.

The speaker's detached. There are nine in the family, but she's divided them into camps of four and four.

In the end both sides seem part of nature because of words like *human alarm clock* and *biological time clocks.* Both sides belong together if only for the comedy of their togetherness: images of sleeping sisters by the TV, Father running the vacuum, while someone rattles pots and pans cooking huge breakfasts for both camps.

7

Hindsight (Chapter 30)

EAT MAMALA, EAT

Because my grandma always said "Eat mamala, eat," I eat a lot today. Had she only told me to eat at meal times the effect might not have been so bad; but because she prescribed food whenever I was frustrated by things not going the way I'd like, I sit here now, struggling with this essay, pen in one hand and a pizza in the other.

Grandma was a round, lovable woman who we called Bubby. She lived with my parents, my brother and sister and I. She seemed to live solely for us. Bubby sewed clothes for us and played with us, but more than anything else she was the cook of our house. It was an arrangement that she and my mom (who couldn't cook to save herself) had since before I was born.

Cooking was definitely Bubby's forte. I didn't really think so at the time. In fact I ate many a meal just to please her. Although I was very young at the time and couldn't express it, I knew that cooking was very important to her. I think it was the one tangible thing that she knew she did for us. She did so much more though. The time she spent with me was priceless. But to Bubby providing the meals was an accomplishment; a measurable way to show her love and her worth. So how could I show her I loved her? Eating was one obvious way.

I was the youngest child in my family. My mother would be busy getting my brother and sister off to school, making the beds, doing the wash, etc. while Bubby and I would go through our morning ritual. First she always took the time to cut *shticlech* for me. *Shticlech* were tiny triangular buttered rye bread sandwiches; just the perfect size for a preschooler's tiny mouth. Then we would play school. Bubby was my built-in play mate. She was illiterate, which made me feel very smart. I would try to teach her to read words that I had memorized like *dog* and *cat*. When she failed to learn, I'd say "Bubby, go to the corner!": she always complied.

Play time went into lunch time. I paid Bubby back for her time by eating.

Sometimes Bubby would help my mom clean. I remember her

waxing the floors on her hands and knees. Her eyes were so bad though that she'd over wax them and my mom would have a fit. So Bubby eventually stuck strictly to cooking.

Dinners came and went. I usually hated them but I did my best for Bubby.

As I got older, when the things of life got me down she always lent me an ear: I didn't even have to ask. After listening to my tale of woe, she would say, "Let me fix you something to eat, you'll feel better." I can remember her saying it one time after I'd quarrelled with my mother and then taken my bad mood out on her. I said, "I'm sorry I yelled at you Bubby, but Mommy made me feel bad." She said, "Ich fershteist, Mamala (i.e.: I understand), let me get you something to eat." I had a bowl of Cheerios and milk and did feel better. The feeling better didn't come from the food though, but as a by-product of making amends for yelling at her.

The food itself never made me feel good. It made Bubby feel good, and that made me happy. She's gone now. I'd love to have her with me still. How she and my little preschooler would enjoy playing school.

I'd love a batch of Bubby's *varenicas* to see me through a week of finals now too; funny I didn't appreciate her cooking then. And some of her apple strudel would have been fine last winter when I was stuck in the house for what seemed like forever, as each of my children took a turn at having the chicken pox.

I do eat a lot and much more than necessary. I eat when I'm frustrated by things not going the way I'd like. This assignment helped me to realize that it was the subconscious memory of my precious grandmother's voice saying, "Eat mamala, eat," and her obvious delight when I did, that has caused my overeating habit today.

Joanne Nizzo

Observations

1. Joanne shows herself as a child in a little series of events with her grandmother. She names delicious moments of food and tells us how much of their flavor was in her willingness to please, her sense of gratefulness to her good grandmother who cooked for her and saw the gift of food as answer or compensation for frustrations other than hunger. The unifying thread is the power of loving exchange. The wonderful picture of literate preschool child and illiterate grandmother playing school dissolved into reversed values at the stroke of 12 as at noon Grandma is the grown-up cook and Joanne the child gratefully waiting to be fed.

The essay ends with a little coda of cause and effect. The image of the lost grandmother modifies and sweetens somewhat the dissatisfaction latent in Joanne's description of her own present attitude to eating.

2. The essay centers around an analysis, stated then developed through a series of images. At first it's a simple cause-and-effect. But as memories of her grandmother unfold, we see there's more than overeating involved.

Interesting relationship of the youngest and the oldest who resemble each other in their states of ignorance, dependence, and sometimes being in the wrong. The grandmother gets much larger than a simple cause. We see her making a life for herself as best she can with her strengths: cooking, playfulness, service, sympathy.

The essay keeps bringing images and memories to the present time of the writing of the essay. We see Joanne first in the two roles of her memory images: pencil in one hand (still a student) and pizza in the other. A third role emerges in the course of the essay: she is also a mother of pre-schoolers, but she has to be "Bubby" too and be patient and serving.

So the essay turns out not to be about how Bubby affected her eating habits but about how much Bubby taught her about doing all you can with what you are? Or about how receiving can be as loving as giving? But the writer keeps the focus on the grandmother and returns to the simple cause-and-effect statement of the beginning.

8

Foresight (Chapter 32)

THE NIGHT WE DRIED SETH OUT

I thought, "There's no way I can let Seth drive home in his condition." Yet I realized that my inebriated uncle was not likely to take a thirteen-year-old's warning very seriously.

My Bar Mitzvah celebration had been perfect. It was a beautiful Sunday in the spring of 1978, and about a hundred people had attended the party, held in the back yard of my home. Towards the end of the party, I overheard my mother say to my father, "What a silly kid that Seth is. He's in no condition to drive, so I guess we'll have to put him up for the night."

Seth, my mother's youngest sibling, is only four years older than I am. He had been in a festive mood that day, and had imbibed half a bottle of champagne. I joined my parents' conversation.

"Seth's a terrific guy," I said, defending my best friend. "His one fault is that he gets a bit carried away at parties when the wine is served. So let's try not to make mountains out of molehills."

"Save the clichés for your English essays," my mother replied with a smile. She then got back to the point. "It's not that Seth is such a bad guy, it's just that he sometimes does weird things. Take today: we invite him to a formal celebration, and what does he wear? Levis and his 'Kiss me, I'm a psychology major' T-shirt!"

I grinned. "Forgetting about his casual attire, Mom, you've got to admit that your brother's got brains. He's been on the dean's list for the past two semesters. He'd never be stupid enough to get behind the wheel in his condition!"

My mother nodded. "Seth is a bit immature, but he's no fool," she seemed to be thinking.

"Hey, look who's coming," I said to her. "Hi, Seth. How did you enjoy the party?"

He talked quite well despite his impaired state, although his unsteady gait gave him away. "I had a terrific time," he replied. "I guess I'd better be going now."

My mother burst out laughing. "That Seth, he's such a joker! Imagine his driving home now!" Seth shot her a puzzled look, and I nudged her with my elbow.

"He's serious!" I whispered. Then I turned to my uncle. "Listen, Seth, if you could just stay for another few minutes and help us clean up, we'd really appreciate it."

My uncle was not very helpful, carrying chairs into the house at the rate of five an hour, but I was at least buying time.

"I'd better tell Seth to stay here for the night," my mother said with a concerned look on her face. "He's had his driver's license for only six months and he's the only brother I've got!"

"He isn't going to listen to his older sister," I pointed out. "Don't forget, Mom, he's still an adolescent!"

"Then I'll advise him as a physician," she countered. "He would certainly follow doctor's orders!"

I shook my head. "Your approach is too risky. He mustn't think that we doubt his ability to drive or he'll get behind the wheel before you can say 'drunk driver.' The best approach would be to get him to stay overnight by some other means."

"You're right," my mother nodded. "I'll invite him to stay."

"If it's all right, I'd prefer to handle this myself," I said slowly. My mother seemed to be hesitating. "I really think I can convince Seth not to leave, and I assure you that if he tries to go, I'll call you immediately."

My mother finally agreed, and I now pondered exactly what to do. Telling Seth outright that he was drunk would only be taken as a challenge. He'd ask himself, "Who's smarter? A thirteen-year-old or me?" Besides, telling him outright was exactly what I had told my mother would be self-defeating. No, I would have to be creative.

"Seth," I asked him, "We really didn't get to spend much time together. How about staying overnight?"

He yawned. "Maybe some other time."

At that point I really got scared. For the first time, it looked like I was going to fail in my simple mission. I broke the silence by suddenly sneezing. "Does anyone have a tissue?" I asked through a stuffed nose.

My uncle pointed to his jacket, which was slung over a chair. "Left pocket," he said.

As I reached inside his pocket, I felt something among the tissues. It was a key chain! Glancing nervously at Seth, I pocketed the keys. I left the room and quietly removed the key labeled "G.M." I then returned the keys to my uncle's jacket. "I might as well have some insurance that he's not going anywhere!" I thought with a smile.

I realized that I hadn't completed my task yet. Seth would soon notice the missing key. That is, unless I got him to stay of his own free will.

"I really should be going now," he suddenly said.

I knew I had to do something. "All right," I said. "But I'm coming with you. I'm off tomorrow, and I haven't been to your apartment in ages. Just give me ten minutes to pack a suitcase."

"Hey, that's right," Seth smiled. "It's Memorial Day tomorrow. Okay, Daniel, I'll wait for you, but please make it quick."

He lay down on the couch, ignoring the dozen coats he was crushing. I went into my room and began to "pack" very slowly. After ten minutes had passed, and Seth hadn't told me to hurry up, I began to suspect that we were going to have an overnight house guest. I walked into the den, and my suspicions were confirmed. Seth was fast asleep, snoring loudly enough to disturb the entire block. He did not wake up as the last of the guests pulled their coats from under him.

The next morning Seth woke up, completely sober, complaining only of a mild headache. He seemed quite annoyed at my mother. "Do you realize that I almost drove home with enough alcohol in my blood to open a liquor store? You could at least have tried to stop me. If I hadn't fallen asleep, who knows what might have happened?"

My mother, valiantly keeping a straight face, apologized. We both knew that a drunk Seth would not have reacted so rationally. Only with a great deal of diplomacy and deception, not to mention an act of petty larceny just to be sure, were we able to keep my uncle from endangering his life and the lives of others.

Because of the above experience, my family no longer serves alcoholic beverages when we throw a party. If a guest brings a bottle of brandy, my father will graciously thank him, but will then put the bottle in the liquor cabinet for future use. The guest may be slightly offended when we serve Coca-Cola or iced tea instead of his gift, but perhaps he'd be more understanding after reading this essay.

Daniel Balsam

Observations

1. The whole essay is written in dialogue. The dialogue is like a drama (shows character in speech and acts) and like a debate (about the most diplomatic way to do something).

It's interesting that Daniel has two purposes: drying Seth out, and getting older people to agree to let him handle it. The effort of a 13-year-old to handle a grown-up situation coincides with the celebration of his initiation as an adult.

Lots of language about family relationships. Each relationship has two terms for it because each is seen from two points of view: Seth is kid brother but also older uncle; mother is also sister; son is also nephew. But there are other names for these same people and they bring in another, larger social and professional world: mother is physician; Seth is student of psychology.

It's funny that the student of psychology is out-psychologized by his nephew.

Most noticeable is the tact or consideration of the relationships. No one embarrasses Seth before or after the crisis. The mother even apologizes for Seth's folly. We see she probably has ideas about Daniel's attempt that she doesn't express.

There's a play of wit throughout the essay, both in thinking and in humor. Seth's condition could go two ways: he could fall asleep or he could have a car accident. So the actual outcome seems not forced but "logical."

Best of all, Seth is really rescued by his own kindliness. He doesn't mind being the "best friend" of a younger boy, and it was his offer of friendly hospitality to Daniel that enabled Daniel's reasonableness to succeed. So the harmony of social good will actually preserves Seth from committing a dangerously anti-social act. The essay ends by bringing in that larger social world suggested earlier by the words *physician, psychology,* and by the religious ritual.

2. The story Daniel tells is concrete all the way, letting us hear his dialogues with himself, his mother, and his uncle. The problem shows up twice, once in the simple form of "We can't let Seth drive," and again as it's mediated by the special concern Daniel feels for the honor and independent integrity—as well as the safety—of his admired Dean's-list uncle. In the second form Daniel shows us step by step what's acceptable and what's intolerable to the high standards of invisibility he sets to his goal of interference. We're in suspense as his options narrow. Details prolong the suspense. Anxiety isn't dissipated until the definer of the delicacy of the problem, Daniel, chooses to absent himself artfully, and Seth resolves the problem by falling asleep.

The circumstantial evidence of the problem suggests the larger effect of the incident, though that's stated more succinctly. The voice of the speaker is maintained as he lists the steps of his family's program for future celebrations.

9

Insight (Chapter 33)

WRONG PLACE, WRONG TIME

Oh God! He wants me to go with him to Louisiana. Where the hell is Louisiana? For a second I pictured myself beating clothes against a rock by a river while Scott was hunting for squirrel. Was that how it would be? He was asking me to make a decision, one that would affect me like no other before. I chose not to leave my home because I simply was not ready to give up my childhood.

At fifteen I was madly in love with him; at sixteen I was dating him. Now I was seventeen, and he wanted me to move away with him. Of course, I would go. Isn't that the way I always heard it should be? The man you love whisks you away to some distant land where you struggle to make a home for yourself in the wilderness. Wasn't this everything I've always wanted? So why was I hesitating? It would be wonderful. Scott would go fishing and hunting; I was used to that. And I would stay home and, well, do whatever it was women did at home. Then, when he came home, we would be happy together, and I would cook dinner, and we would make love. Oh, yes, it would be so nice, just like the songs on the radio.

Who was I kidding? I would go crazy. I would be miserable out in the woods with no friends and family. And how would we make a living? How would I deal with the southern mentality, or even better, how would they deal with us? I had never lived with a man before. Was what I heard true? Would he change? Even worse, could he change, deal with me being around all the time? I was going crazy with all these thoughts running through my mind, and suddenly it became clear. I didn't have to look ahead 15 years—just one year to see myself as a child in a grown-up world. I couldn't do it. Yes, I wanted him, but here in New York with me the way it always was.

At seventeen I was still a child, not a baby, but aware enough to know I wouldn't fit into a world of vacuum cleaners and Sunday morning washes. I couldn't handle the responsibility and knew that trying to play house would only hurt us both in the end. That was my whole problem; it would only be a game, something that I knew would end if I ever wanted it to. Maybe that's why I could never start, because in the game of love and commitment there wasn't supposed to be an end, only an ever-after.

When I realized that my only decision could be no, I faced it. It would have been so easy to fool myself. After all, I was in love. Wasn't I? But there were too many doubts, even doubts about him that I never knew existed before. I was too young and too scared to pick up and leave everything I had become so accustomed to. This wasn't merely a question of love but one that could affect the rest of my life. I had to ask myself if our relationship could compensate for everything I was giving up. The answer was, it couldn't, and if I said *no* now it would be better than two or three years from now when we were both miserable and resentful.

The day I told him, for a few seconds I was paralyzed. How after all I had gone through with him, how could I say *no*? But I did, and now it all seems like it was so long ago and it doesn't even matter anymore; and yet, then it mattered so much.

Elizabeth Drew

Observations

1. Elizabeth opens with immediacy of dialogue and a delightful setting. Then the snake in this Eden: the need to decide. She catches a glimpse of herself as romantic heroine—or rather of him as romantic hero, herself admiring him somewhere close by. The first note of doubt is a beautifully placed "well": "I, well, I would do whatever it is women do." The romantic dream has a breach in it, and she's found it.

Then come the questions. A middle section shows her tossing them around. "Will he change?" modulates into another question in which she is the object. Then she looks at herself, her age, her unwillingness to play house or love. The bit-by-bit method of stating the problem as it occurred, then opening out the parts of it till she strikes the one crucial part—herself—suggests her intensity. By the end of the middle part she goes from looking down a long vista of years to looking at herself at that moment.

So convincing is her rehearsal of the dilemma and its resolution that I was surprised to learn at the end that it was an issue long resolved, not recent as I'd thought, hearing it so freshly told. I was moved to hear the last words tell me it doesn't matter any more at all, the once sharply pointed dilemma which poignantly mattered then. I heard in that sentence a remote echo of the girl who said, "I, well, whatever" at the beginning—the passionate realist.

2. There's a striking contrast between how hard and painful was the decision (most of the essay), and how remote it seems now: "It doesn't even matter any more." Nothing mediates the extremes of the two times: when it mattered so much and when not at all.

Most of the essay is presented as the decision takes place. It's interesting that she begins thinking about it with a fantasy of delight. Fantasy bumps up against a hard question right in the midst of fantasy, and that starts a string of hard questions.

I notice that several questions were about what others would make of her—as well as what she would do with them. She sees how she would be part of the problem.

She expresses her decision partly in images (vacuum cleaners and Sunday morning washes) and partly in terms of thought: words like *responsibility, commitment*. The whole essay does that—keeps images right along with thought-words, abstract words.

She defines love seriously—commitment—and in contrast to that going to Louisiana would be a game. Then I notice that she doesn't disvalue *game* either, but just accepts herself as a child. Her reasoning is gone through and defined in a slightly different language about three times. That suggests she had it well in mind. She didn't say *no* because it didn't matter, but because it mattered more than a child could sustain.

Appendix

Two Designs
for a Writing Course

When You Work with Others on Writing

1. **Begin work at once.**
    Promptness is the reality of your sense of purpose. Agree on a meeting time and begin on the moment. (Lateness is the concern of the latecomer.)

2. **Write in every meeting.**
    Conduct your meetings by writing. This book (as no other book does) gives you a set of ways to learn writing directly, by writing.

3. **Expect good things from everyone but not the same things.**
    Neither you nor I can know how a writer will or should develop a writing assignment. It's sometimes hard to believe, but there's no best or right way to compose an assignment. All writing is literary creation, unique and various, and can't be analyzed ahead of time.

4. **Begin work directly, without introductions, explanations, or analysis.**
    Analysis is the reorganizer. It can't bring the body to life.

5. **Describe the writing you hear.**
    No mental work can begin or progress using judgmental terms.

6. **Work from strength.**
    Tasks develop mastery when they aim at ripening functions—are oriented not to weaknesses but to strengths.

*   *   *

You can practice the elements of writing well by starting with the work in Chapter 1 and keeping going. This book is planned to carry you forward in good order. What follows now is just a sample, showing in detail two of a number of possible designs for scheduling the work. It's divided to reflect how long the parts take, and to distinguish parts you'll do in the presence of others from parts you'll do on your own.

The big general notion of the design is: Keep writing; keep reading; keep going. Shape your sessions to a forward rhythm. It will sustain you even if you're tired or preoccupied. A slack, interrupted pace falls into shambles. Coherent shapes—sentences, literary forms, and group meetings—are networks for fluent energy.

A small useful notion is: Keep order as your writing accumulates. Label and date each piece as you do it.

1. Elements of the Essay

This sample design is for a group of 10-20 persons, meeting twice a week (A and B below) for 75 minutes, during 14 weeks.

Week 1

1A. Take 15 minutes to go round the group and learn each other's names.

Read Chapter 5. When it tells you to write, do so at once.

Read each person's work aloud.

Assignment: Read Chapters 1-5.

Write again, step by step, from the directions in Chapter 5.

1B. Read your new work aloud. Notice, as you listen, how you wait for the last satisfying sentences.

After all have read, write down any last sentences you can remember. Put lots of them on the blackboard if you have one.

Assignment: Read over all of Chapter 5.

Write Fable 3. Remember that the wit of great fables is brief, and put in only the words you need.

Read Chapter 18 thoughtfully.

Week 2

2A. As described in Chapter 8, write nonstop for 10 minutes.

Read your nonstop prolific writing aloud.

Move into small groups. Shift seats with Olympic quickness. Promptly read Fable 3 aloud.

Tear off 2 bits of paper. Write the name of an animal on each. Put the papers in a pile. Let each pick 2 for use as characters in Fable 4.

Assignment: Read Chapter 8.

Write Fable 4, using characters picked by luck in the last session.

Write nonstop for 10 minutes. Do this every day for the rest of 14 weeks (and, at best, for the rest of your life).

If you're ambitious, or if you're not a native English-speaker, increase prolific-writing time to 15 minutes. It's the best way to confirm and extend your grammar-power.

2B. One person reads Fable 4 aloud. Choose 1 of its 3 aphorisms, a good one, and copy it.

As described in Chapter 6, in 5 minutes nonstop, rewrite the aphorism in 3-5 new versions.

Read the new sentences aloud. If there's a blackboard, fill it as each of you copies the rewrite you like best.

Still in small groups, read one piece of your prolific writing aloud.

Assignment: Write Fable 5.

Continue prolific writing daily, of course.

Read Chapter 6 carefully. Look over Chapter 7. You'll be working from it next time.

Week 3

3A. Read Fable 5 aloud.

Choose a fable from the work so far. Read it aloud. Invent 3 new aphorisms for it by writing nonstop for 5 minutes.

As described in Chapter 7, read these aloud. Choose one. Copy it. Write for 3 minutes nonstop on what you notice about how it's written.

Read these observations aloud.

Take 5 minutes and write nonstop on the new experience of writing what you notice. Read these aloud.

Assignment: Write Fable 6. Rewrite it to make it shine with elegance. Keep it brief.

Reread Chapter 7.

Use a daily prolific-writing time to say what you notice about writing from this book. Try to do this once a week from now on.

Read Chapter 41.

3B. Read Fable 6 aloud.

Choose a fable to reread aloud. Write 3-5 new aphorisms for it, in 5 minutes nonstop. Read them aloud.

Pick a new aphorism; copy it; rewrite it 3 times into sentences which convey the same thought in new language. Read these aloud. (This simplest form of rewriting rewriting has rare power. It's one of the few known ways to reach a frame of mind where new ideas are likely. Note that some new aphorism develop the original one, and some use it as the jump-off place for the leap to new insight. Rewrite rewriting whenever you want to think for yourself.)

Assignment: Choose one aphorism from each of your Fables 1-5. Rewrite each in at least 3 versions.

Read Chapters 9 and 13.

Week 4

4A. In small groups, read Fable 6 aloud.

Choose and read aloud the sentence you like best of the 15 + you wrote at home. Pick one you've heard and copy it. Rewrite it in 3 versions. Read these aloud.

For 5 minutes, write nonstop about these sentences and the way they work: as simple assertions, or in balanced coordination, or ordered by subordinating one idea to another. (Always copy sentences you like into your notebook.)

Choose another aphorism and do it all again as above.

Assignment: Choose your favorite of your fables. Rewrite it to be as brief and bright as possible. Using ditto, carbon, or Xerox, make enough copies for each person in the group.

You'll work on Chapter 10 next time.

4B. Read Chapter 10. Write nonstop as it directs, about family stories.

Read the results aloud.

Write again. (This second writing is vital!) Read aloud as many as you've time for.

Distribute copies of your chosen fable. Each now has a personal copy of your group's new anthology of fables.

Assignment: Choose one of your stories, and write Parable 1.

Use 2-3 of your next daily nonstop sessions to write notes, with your observations about their work, to 3 of the authors in your group's new anthology.

Read Chapter 13 again, carefully.

Week 5

5A. Read Parable 1 aloud in turn, right around the group.

Have someone reread a parable. Write nonstop for 5 minutes to say what you notice about it.

Read these notes to the authors.

Deliver your notes about their fables to the authors.

Assignment: Choose another story. Tell it in full, for Parable 2.

Read Chapters 9 and 18 again.

Use a daily prolific-writing time to write on your experience with grammar.

5B. In small groups, read Parable 2. Listen; after each, write and read your observations.

Jot notes on family stories you recall as you hear others read.

Read your prolific writing on your experience with grammar.

Assignment: Choose another story. Tell it in full, for Parable 3.

Don't forget to review your work as a writer, now and then, in your daily prolific writing.

Reread Chapter 9 to make sure you know what it says.

Week 6

6A. In small groups, read Parable 3. Listen; after each, write and read your observations. (In this bare schedule, the procedure may sound monotonous. But — as you now know — it sets up a crisp rhythm you can count on. It keeps you going forward and gives you what all writers deserve, an attentive and responsive hearing.)

Pick a good sentence from one of the parables read so far. Copy it. Rewrite it in 3 versions; read these aloud. Admire them. And keep in mind the power of rewriting to discover ideas. Use it all the time.

Assignnment: Freshen your supply of ideas by writing nonstop on "the story of..."as described in Chapter 10. Write Parable 4.

Read all your prolific writing to see what you like. Use 10 minutes of daily writing to plan future prolific writing: will you try rough drafts? letters? general craziness? progress reports? It's up to you. Like rewriting rewriting, writing nonstop opens your mind to emerging new ideas of your own.

You'll be using Chapter 11 next time.

6B. Have someone read a parable aloud. Think about the behavior of the main character.

Write, nonstop, 4-6 adjectives, as described in Chapter 11. Read the adjectives aloud. Select the most fitting. Change it into a noun. Use that noun as the subject of a sentence, followed by "is," as directed. You need to write at least 2 such sentences. Read all the sentences aloud.

With another parable, do it all again. Put a sentence from each person on the blackboard if you have one.

Assignment: Write 5 adjectives suited to the main character in your Parable 4. Choose the best one; transform it into a noun; use the noun as the subject of 3 sentences.

Repeat this with another of your parables.

Read Chapters 11 and 12.

Week 7

7A. Have 2 people read Parable 4, the adjective, and the noun derived from it, then their sentences begun with that noun. Choose one of these sentences. Copy it.

Have the parable it fits read again. Write 3 sentences that follow from the one you copied; tell more about the noun, and move in the direction of the parable. Read these aloud, including the sentence you copied.

Do it again.

Assignment: Develop one of the sentences you wrote for your own Parable 4, as described in Chapter 11.

Read Chapter 12 again.

7B.   In small groups, read Parable 4 and the paragraph of sentences derived from it. Quickly write and read your observations about each.

As a whole group, have someone read: first a paragraph, then the parable it came from. Ask for a second reading if you like. Now write a new paragraph to show how the story has developed the sense of the first paragraph. Read these new paragraphs aloud. Have the author read again: the first paragraph beginning with a noun + the parable + the new paragraph derived from both. It's an essay with beginning, middle, and end.

Assignment: For another of your parables, begin with a list of adjectives and work through the process described in Chapter 12, to write Essay 1.

Week 8

8A.   Copy this: "An expository sentence supports the idea it asserts." Remember it. Use it to test every essay you write, by asking, "Do I have an idea? Have I plainly asserted it? Have I supported it firmly?"

Read Essay 1 around the room.

Find another family story by writing nonstop for 10 minutes. Read as many as there's time for.

Assignment: Write Essay 2, using a new family parable, as described in Chapter 12.

You're now over half way through this course, in which you're writing your own text. Use a daily prolific-writing stint to say what your text looks like to you.

Reread Chapter 13 to refresh your powers of observation. Read Chapter 23.

8B.   Read, in the whole group, 3 examples of Essay 2. Listen. Write and read observations on each essay. Jot down observations you hear which you might use for your next essay or your rewriting of this one.

Assignment: Read over all your parables. Choose one, rewrite it, and make a good fair copy. Provide enough copies to give one to each member of your group.

Read Chapters 9 and 18 again.

Week 9

9A. Have someone read a good opening sentence from Essay 2. Copy it. Rewrite it in 3 versions. *Keep the abstracted first word, but place it anywhere in the sentence and follow it with any verb.* Make it elegant, an original assertion of a personal definition. Read the sentences aloud.

Choose a rewritten sentence. Copy it; write 10 minutes nonstop on any experience it calls to mind. Read these aloud.

Distribute copies of your parable, so you all have copies of the group's anthology.

Assignment: Starting with a sentence you rewrote last time, compose a 3-part essay, Essay 3. For the middle, rewrite the description of an experience which you wrote nonstop during the last session. Or, try more prolific free writing to find one you like better.

Note how useful this combination of prolific writing and re-writing rewriting is for rummaging through your mind.

9B. In small groups, read Essay 3. Write and read observations about each.

Make sure you stick to reading observations as you have written them. Don't use them as a springboard for improvising.

Still in small groups, choose and read a piece of your prolific writing. After all have read, write observations nonstop for 10 minutes. Read these aloud.

Assignment: Write Essay 4, following directions in Chapter 12: begin with concrete expression, discover your idea; develop and arrange your support; conclude. But write the concluding paragraph on a separate piece of paper.

You'll be working on Chapter 14 next time. Also read Chapter 19.

Week 10

10A. Following directions in Chapter 14, have someone read the beginning and middle of an Essay 4. Read it twice. Write and read observations. Write 5-10 sentences as a fitting conclusion. Read these aloud.

Do it again. Read another Essay 4 up to the ending. Write and read observations. Write 5-10 concluding sentences.

Exchange the beginning and middle of your Essay 4 with a colleague. Hold on to your ending.

Assignment: Read and reread your colleague's essay. Put it aside; write observations nonstop for 10 minutes. Write 5-10 sentences as a conclusion.

Write Essay 5, following directions in Chapter 12, as for Essay 4.

Read Chapter 15. You'll be working on it next time.

10B. Read and write from directions in Chapter 15 on the pronoun, "I." Read the results aloud.

In small groups, read Essay 5 aloud. As you write and read observations, pay special heed to endings.

Give back your colleague's paper and your conclusion to it.

Read over your own Essay 4, including your colleague's and your own conclusions. Rewrite your conclusion, using both as inspiration.

Assignment: During the next week, write about 8 more pronouns, as described in Chapter 15. Use daily prolific-writing time if you like.

Read Chapters 16 and 19.

Write 3 sentences about each of 3 abstract nouns in Chapter 19. Begin with the noun, and follow it with "is."

Week 11

11A. Choose from the sentences you've prepared the one you like best. Copy it, and in 50 minutes write a 3-part essay, Essay 6. Read Chapter 16. Follow its directions, and rewrite the beginning of one of your essays.

Assignment: Write Essay 7, using another of the sentences you prepared for last time. (Rewrite it first, of course.)

Keep up your research on pronouns as in Chapter 15.

11B. Read Essay 7 aloud in small groups. Write and read observations; pay heed to beginnings and endings.

Rewrite the beginning of Essay 7, following directions in Chapter 16.

Assignment: Choose another abstract noun from the list in Chapter 19. Write a 3-part essay based on it. Stick to a 50-minute limit.

Read Chapter 17. You'll be using it next time.

Finish your 9-page research on your use of pronouns, as described in Chapter 15.

Week 12

12A. In small groups, read Chapter 17.

Follow the steps in Chapter 17 and rewrite the middle of Essay 8. Your data — the material of your support — are your experiences.

Read your work on the pronoun "we" aloud. Consider using "we" and "I" in your next essay.

Assignment: Read Chapter 19 on writing based on concrete words. Choose 3 words from the list; write 3 sentences for each.

Write Essay 9, in 50 minutes. Use one of the 3 sentences to begin it.

Try using daily prolific writing for something wild now and then. (Look over Chapter 8 again.)

12B. In small groups, read Essay 9. Write and read observations.

Using one of the concrete words listed in Chapter 19, write Essay 10 in no more than 50 minutes.

Assignment: Read Chapter 20. Following the directions carefully, use one of the quotations as the basis, and write Essay 11.

Week 13

13A. In small groups, read Essay 11 aloud. Write and read observations.

Write beginning paragraphs for the remaining 5 quotations in Chapter 20.

Continue to follow directions for working with a quotation. Read the paragraphs aloud.

Assignment: Choose a beginning you wrote last time. Rewrite it as your first paragraph, and write Essay 12.

13B. Rewrite another of the beginnings you wrote last time. Write Essay 13 based on it. Stick to 50 minutes.

Assignment: Choose the essay you like best so far. Rewrite it top to bottom. Make a fair copy. Provide enough copies for the whole group.

Week 14

14A. Read the rewritten essays right around the room. Write and read observations.

Distribute copies, so that you have your copy of the group's anthology of good essays.

Assignment: Write as many more practice essays as you can. Limit them strictly to 50 minutes.

14B. Write a 50-minute essay on an unrehearsed assigned subject, as a test of how far you've come.

2. Two-Part Essay Shapes

This design is for a group of 20-25 writers, meeting twice a week for 75 minutes, during 14 weeks. Timing depends on a brisk, steady rhythm of working, but here's a fact to help you adjust the size of the group to the amount of work it does. One page of typing double-spaced is about 250 words. It takes two minutes to read. The first-version or core essays for this course are about 250-300 words, so 20 people can read core essays in about 40 minutes.

Be sure to make a copy for yourself of all your assigned writing. (We recommend carbon paper because it's cheap and very convenient.) You hand in *all* assigned writing (except what you write in your daily nonstop writing sessions); and because you commonly work again right away on this writing, you must have your own copy.

The work in the group gives priority to reading new work aloud and to practicing new techniques or new kinds of writing together.

Week 1

1A. This is one way to learn each other's names right away: the Grandma Game, a parlor game our grandparents played to get acquainted at parties. It goes this way: Iris begins and says, "My grandmother went to California and brought back ice for Iris." Molly, sitting next to her, says, "My grandmother went to California and brought back money for Molly and ice for Iris." Tom, next, says, "My grandmother went to California and brought back timber for Tom, money for Molly, and ice for Iris." So it goes around the room. Should anyone falter, everyone helps; it's not a game to win or lose. Our group will be a community not a competition. We notice how easy it is for everyone to pay attention to the same thing, how laughing goes with learning.

Follow the directions in Chapter 5 step by step to write a dialogue. Read each person's work aloud.

Do it again: write a second dialogue and read them aloud.

Assignment: Read Chapters 1 through 5. Write again, step by step, from the directions in Chapter 5: Fable 3.

Read Chapter 6.

1B. Read your new fables aloud. Recall aphorisms you enjoyed and ask authors to read them again so that you can copy them down.

Choose one aphorism and rewrite it in three versions, following directions in Chapter 6. Read the rewritten aphorisms aloud.

Do it again: choose another aphorism, rewrite it in 3 versions, and read them aloud. Have writers put their brightest sentences on the board.

Read Chapter 8. Reread Chapter 6. Choose one aphorism from each of your three fables written so far. Rewrite each aphorism in at least 4 versions. (A total of 12 aphorisms)

Read Chapter 9.

Week 2

2A. As described in Chapter 8, write nonstop for 10 minutes. Read this prolific writing aloud.

Ask each writer to read one aphorism from the 12 rewritten aphorisms. Choose one from those you hear, copy it (ask the author to read it again if necessary). Rewrite it in 3 versions. Read these aloud.

For 5 minutes write nonstop about how these sentences work as simple assertions, balanced coordination, or by subordinating one idea to another. Read these sentence analyses aloud.

Assignment: Write Fable 4 beginning with animal dialogue written step by step. (Don't give the animals names, which makes them pets instead of animal types, and remember not to begin with a preconceived moral or a familiar story.)

Reread Chapter 8. As described there, write nonstop for 15 minutes. Do this every day for the rest of the 14 weeks.

Read Chapter 7.

2B. Ask one writer to read Fable 4. Invent 3 new aphorisms for it and read them aloud. Choose one, copy it, and write observations on it nonstop for 3 minutes. (This is described in Chapter 7.) Read these observations aloud. Listen appreciatively, without interruption.

Do it again for another aphorism.

Assignment: Write Fable 5. Rewrite it to make it as concise and elegant as possible.

Read Chapter 18. Use one of your daily nonstop writing sessions to write about your experience with grammar.

Read Chapters 22 and 23.

Week 3

3A. As described in Chapter 23, write for 5 minutes nonstop a list of seed sentences for Once/Now. Read these sentences aloud.

Choose your best sentence and write for 10 minutes nonstop about the *Once* part of the sentence.

Now write for 10 minutes nonstop on the *Now* part of the sentence.

If time allows, read some of your prolific writing accounts of your experience with grammar.

Assignment: Write to expand both parts of the essay you began in the group so that you have the core of an essay, about 250-300 words: Essay 1, Once/Now.

Read Chapters 7 and 13. Read Chapter 23 again.

3B. Read all the essays aloud. Recall one and have its author read it again. As described in Chapter 13 (and as you did for the aphorism), write nonstop for 5 minutes what you notice about the way the essay is written. Read these observations aloud and listen without interruption.

As described at the end of Chapter 23, write to expand your rewritten seed sentence into an ample first paragraph.

Assignment: Read Chapter 15. Read Chapter 12. As described there, write a new final paragraph for Essay 1.

Read Chapters 18 and 9 again.

Rewrite Fables 1-4 to make them shine. Copy edit your fables to make sure the punctuation of dialogue is correct. Check back to Chapter 5 for a sample of dialogue. Make a fair copy of your fables. Proofread them to make sure they match your copy-edited, correct copy.

Use one of your daily writing sessions to write more seed sentences for Once/Now.

Week 4

4A. Choose a Fable to reread aloud. Write 3-5 new aphorisms for it in 5 minutes nonstop. Read them aloud.

Choose one of your new aphorisms and copy it. Rewrite it 3 times in new language which conveys the same thought. Read these aloud and listen with appreciation to the beautiful sentences you'll hear. Note the special power of this rewriting rewriting.

As described in Chapter 15, write about the pronoun "I." Read as many of these as time allows.

Assignment: Write another Once/Now essay, Essay 2, in its two part form. (Be sure you're numbering each essay and dating it.)

Continue your pronoun research by writing on the pronouns "we," and "you," as described in Chapter 15.

Read Chapter 26. Read Chapter 41.

4B. Read Essay 2 aloud.

As described in Chapter 26, write seed sentences for the essay "They Say," Essay 3. Read these aloud. Choose your best sentence and write for 15 minutes nonstop what "they" say.

Read these aloud as time allows.

Assignment: Finish writing Essay 3, "They Say."

Read Chapter 9 again.

Following the directions in Chapter 15, finish your writing on prounouns.

Read Chapters 7 and 13 again.

Week 5

5A. In small groups read Essay 3 aloud. After each write for 1 minute what you notice about how the essay is written or what you remember most vividly about it. When you have heard all the essays, read your observations to the authors. (Be sure to stick to what you've written instead of using your writing as notes to improvise.)

Quickly reform into a whole group. Write for 5 minutes nonstop on the experience of writing observations. Read this aloud.

Assignment: Read Chapter 23 again. Compose a new beginning paragraph for Essay 2. Read this paragraph. Reread your core essay.

Consider whether your new first paragraph suggests a better ordering or more development of parts of the original essay.

Read Chapter 12. As described there, write a new concluding paragraph for Essay 2, and write it on a separate sheet of paper.

Read Chapter 14. Read Chapter 24.

5B. As described in Chapter 14, ask one author to read the beginning and middle of Essay 2. Have it read again. Write at least 5 sentences to conclude the essay and read these aloud.

Ask another author to read Essay 2 and do it all again.

Exchange essays with a colleague. Keep the paper with your own conclusion on it.

Assignment: Following the directions in Chapter 14, write a new conclusion for your colleague's Essay 2. Do not omit writing observations on the essay first and be sure you set it aside as you write your observations.

Write a new beginning for your Essay 3. Following the directions at the end of Chapter 26, use the question form of the seed sentence to write a new concluding paragraph for your Essay 3.

Week 6

6A. Quickly return your colleague's essay with your own conclusion to it and receive your own. Read your Essay 2 again with your own conclusion and the one written by your colleague. In 15 minutes nonstop rewrite the conclusion, combining the best of both your own and your colleague's paragraphs.

Read aloud the new concluding paragraphs for your Essay 3. Recall a sentence that defines an opposition assumption tellingly and ask the author to read it again. Copy it and rewrite it in 3 versions, keeping the noun that names the assumption. Read these sentences aloud.

Assignment: Refer to your stock of seed sentences for Essay 3 and choose one. Write a new "They Say," Essay 4.

Read Chapters 16 and 17.

As described in Chapter 14, rewrite the conclusion of your Essay 3. Go on to rewrite the beginning and middle. Rewrite your last sentence till it sounds exactly right. Copy-edit it and make a fair copy: well-spelled, neatly punctuated, and intelligently paragraphed. Hand it in for a grade.

Look over Chapter 28.

6B. In small groups read Essay 4 aloud and write 1-minute observations after each. When the essays are read, read the observations aloud. Make notes on your essay of what your listeners noticed about it.

Quickly return to the whole group. As described in Chapter 28, write nonstop for 5 minutes a list of seed sentences for Essay 5, Two Voices. Read them aloud.

Assignment: Choose the best seed sentence and write Essay 5, Two Voices, as a two-part essay. (Be sure to number and date your essays.)

Read Chapters 9 and 18 again.

Read Chapter 8 again and use some of your daily nonstop writing sessions to plan future writing.

Week 7

7A. Have one Essay 5 read aloud. Write observations about it nonstop for 5 minutes. Read them to the author.

Quickly move into small groups of 4 or 5 to read the rest of the essays. Write 3-minute observations of each and read them to the authors. Make notes on your essay of the most interesting and helpful observations about it.

Assignment: Read your Essay 5 thoughtfully. Write a new beginning for it. Look over your notes on the observations of your essay. Read your new first paragraph and consider how your core essay should be ordered, concentrated in some parts, developed in others. Make the changes which seem good to you. Write a new conclusion as described at the end of Chapter 26, but, of course, use the question form of the Two Voices Essay (at the end of Chapter 28).

Read Chapter 41.

7B. Have one Essay 5, Two Voices, read aloud without its final paragraph. Have it read again. In 15 minutes nonstop write a new conclusion for it. Read these aloud.

Have another Essay 5 read aloud and do it all again.

Assignment: Read over your Essay 5. Put it aside and write observations about it for 10 minutes. Reread your essay. Now put it aside and write a second concluding paragraph. Following the directions in Chapters 14, 16, and 17, rewrite Essay 5. Give it a good title. Copy-edit it, make a fair copy of it, and proofread it. Hand it in for a grade.

Read Chapter 29. Bring Essay 2 to your next meeting.

Week 8

8A. Read your Essay 2 with its rewritten final paragraph to yourself. Set it aside and write observations on it for 10 minutes: begin with the most obvious thing about it. Now reread your essay and rewrite it in 50 minutes.

Assignment: Rewrite the first and last sentences of Essay 2 to make them shine. Copy-edit it, make a fair copy, and proofread it. Hand it in for a grade.

Reread your Essay 4 with its notes on observations and its best part and sentences marked. (It's still a core essay.) Reviewing what you've learned from Chapters 12, 13, 14, 16, and 17, complete and rewrite the essay.

Use some of your daily nonstop writing sessions for the next three weeks to make notes on: 1) writing assignments (essays or tests) for your other classes, and 2) reading (assigned or not) of non-fiction prose, reading that interests you such as: travel, nature or environment studies, biography, history, etc. Copy the test or writing assignments and for the reading copy a rich, central quotation of 2 or 3 sentences. Use these daily writing sessions also to write observations of the material on which the tests, essays, or quotations are based. This writing will be part of a future assignment.

Read Chapter 26. Look over Chapter 30.

8B.   As described in Chapter 30, write nonstop for 5 minutes a list of seed sentences for the Essay of Hindsight, Essay 6. Read them aloud. Write for another 5 minutes nonstop to add to your list.

Choose the most attractive sentence and write for 20 minutes nonstop about the source in the past for the pattern you see now. Write as concretely as possible (don't try to cover large periods of the past with a general report). Read these aloud as time allows.

Assignment: Complete the writing of the essay you began in the group, Essay 6, Hindsight. Give it a good title after you've finished it.

Reread it and mark the best places and best sentences. Copy the best sentence and rewrite it in 3 versions. Pick the best of these and rewrite it 3 times in new language which conveys the same thought.

Week 9

9A.   In small groups of 4 or 5 read aloud Essay 6. Write 5-minute observations for each essay. Read them to the authors when all the essays have been read. (Be sure to read what you have written instead of using it as notes for improvising.)

Return quickly to the whole group and have one Essay 6 read again. Write for 3 minutes nonstop to describe the most important thing about the way it's written. Read these aloud.

Assignment: Look over your stock of seed sentences for the Two Voices essay and write another, Essay 7.

Look over Chapters 19, 20, and read Chapter 21. Read Chapter 32.

9B. In small groups read Essay 7, Two Voices aloud. Write 5-minute, nonstop observations, aiming to tell each author the most important thing about the writing. Read these aloud.

Quickly return to the whole group. As described in Chapter 32, write seed sentences for the Essay of Foresight, Essay 8. Read them aloud.

Assignment: Complete the Essay of Foresight, Essay 8.

Write a new beginning and ending for Essay 6, Hindsight. Rewrite the conclusion, paying special attention to the question form of the Essay of Hindsight (end of Chapter 30). Rewrite the beginning.

Read Chapter 17 again. Read Chapter 31.

Week 10

10A. In small groups read Essay 8. Write and read 5-minute observations.

Read the first sentence of Chapter 17 and copy it down. Rewrite it in 3 versions. Read these aloud.

Reread your own Essay 6 silently. Following the directions in Chapter 17, rewrite the middle.

Assignment: Order the parts of Essay 6. Copy-edit it, make a fair copy, and proofread it to hand in for a grade.

Read Chapter 40.

Write a new beginning and conclusion for the Essay of Foresight, Essay 8.

Read Chapter 34. Read Chapter 33.

10B. Following the directions in Chapter 33, write a set of seed sentences for the Essay of Insight, Essay 9. Read these aloud. Quickly add 2 or 3 more seed sentences to your list.

Choose the best sentence and write, in 50 minutes, the Essay of Insight, Essay 9.

Assignment: Read Chapter 40 again.

Read over the notes in your daily writing sessions about your writing (tests or essays) for other courses. Study the overview of the six essay shapes at the end of Chapter 33.

Choose one assignment and write 3 seed sentences for it to express the shape of the idea. (If you have no other courses or writing assignments, choose an essay or article you've enjoyed reading and write a test question for it. Do not choose an editorial. Make your test question sound human.)

Reread the test question section for each of the six essay shapes (Chapter 25 and the end of Chapters 26, 28, 30, 32, 33). Choose your best seed sentence and rewrite it in 3 versions. Write a two-part essay (250-300 words) answering the demands of the assignment, Essay 10.

Limit the essay to the *heart* of your idea; choose the most important thing you have to say. Like all your core essays, this one must be concrete. Recall your pronoun writing and consider using the pronoun "I" as the governing pronoun.

Week 11

11A. Ask someone to read Essay 10 aloud. Write for 5 minutes non-stop to describe for the author the most important thing you notice about how the essay is written. Read these observations aloud.

Have another essay read aloud and do it all again.

Move quickly into small groups to read the other essays aloud. Write 3-5 minute observations and read them aloud.

Assignment: Write a new beginning for Essay 9, Insight. Consider the question form of Insight (at the end of Chapter 33). Write a set of trial sentences (as in Chapter 34) to define the situation. (Chapter 11 is specifically about defining.) Choose the best sentence and rewrite it in 3 versions.

Write another set of trial sentences to define the governing principle. Pick the best sentence of this set and rewrite it in 3 versions. Write a concluding paragraph of 5-10 sentences.

From your daily writing sessions of the last 3 weeks, pick one favorite quotation from your reading. Read Chapter 20.

11B. Read your favorite quotation and copy it. Rewrite the quotation in a sentence or two to say what you see it means. Write nonstop for 30 minutes to say why the passage you quote from your reading is significant to the essay from which you took it and important to you. Essay 11.

Quickly form small groups and read your essays aloud. Write and read observations to tell the authors the most important thing you notice about how the essay is written.

Assignment: As described in Chapters 14, 16, and 17, rewrite Essay 8, Foresight. Copy-edit it, make a fair copy, and proofread it to hand in for a grade.

Reread your Essays 10 and 11. Choose one to develop into a complete essay and do so. Write trial sentences (as described in Chapter 34) in order to write a good opening paragraph of at least 5 sentences which show the reader the whole shape of your idea.

Write a new conclusion which ties together the beginning and the evidence for the idea in the middle. Read Chapter 12 again to renew your sense of the shape of the expository essay.

Week 12

12A. Ask one author to read an expanded Essay 10 or 11. Write 5 minutes nonstop to tell the author the most important thing you noticed about how it's written. Read these observations aloud.

Quickly form small groups to read and observe the rest of the essays.

Assignment: As described in Chapters 14, 16, and 17, rewrite Essay 9, Insight. Copy-edit it, make a fair copy, proofread it to hand in for a grade.

Bring your seed sentences for Essay 6 (Hindsight) to class.

12B. Look over your stock of seed sentences and write Essay 12 (Hindsight) as a core essay. Write a new beginning paragraph in which you name and define the pattern and the source. Write a new concluding paragraph to tie the idea and its evidence together. Allow 50 minutes for this.

Quickly form small groups to read these essays aloud. Write and read observations as time allows.

Assignment: Rewrite Essay 12 to make it as coherent and well-articulated as possible. Copy-edit it, make a fair copy, and proofread it to hand in for a grade.

Read Chapters 39 and 41.

Week 13

13A. Read your rewritten Essay 12 around the room. Write observations and read as many as time allows.

Assignment:Write another Essay of Insight, Essay 13. Write a new beginning and conclusion for it.

13B. In small groups read Essay 13 and write 5-minute observations after each one. Read observations to the authors.

Assignment: Choose another assignment or quotation from the notes in your daily writing sessions and write an essay, 14, as you did before. Be sure the core essay is concrete; on the concreteness of your data depends your definition and development.

Write a new beginning and conclusion for the core essay.

Use some of your daily writing sessions to say what you've discovered during the last 13 weeks about your own writing and the writing of expository essays.

Week 14

14A. In small groups read Essay 14 aloud and write observations to tell their authors the most important thing you noticed about how they are written. Read them aloud.

Assignment: Rewrite Essay 14 thoroughly. Make it as cogent as possible. Copy-edit it, make a fair copy, and proofread it to hand in for a grade.

Bring the complete folder of your essays to your next meeting. Set them in order and be sure they are dated and numbered. Choose your favorite essay.

14B. Read your rewritten Essay 14 around the room and listen to them appreciatively. Ask all writers to read aloud their favorite essays.

* * * * * * * * * * * *

Summary of essays rewritten for a grade: Numbers 3 ("They Say"), 5 (Two Voices), 2 (Once/Now), 6 (Hindsight), 8 (Foresight), 9 (Insight), 12 (Hindsight), 14 (on reading or an assigned topic).

Index